ONWARD SOUTHERN SOLDIERS

RELIGION AND
THE ARMY OF TENNESSEE
IN THE CIVIL WAR

TRACI NICHOLS-BELT
with GORDON T. BELT

Charleston  London

THE
History
PRESS

Published by The History Press
Charleston, SC 29403
www.historypress.net

Front cover: Sunrise Service by Mort Künstler. © 2006 Mort Künstler, Inc. www.mkunstler.com

First published 2011

Manufactured in the United States

ISBN 978.1.60949.374.5

Library of Congress Cataloging-in-Publication Data

Nichols-Belt, Traci.
Onward southern soldiers : religion and the Army of Tennessee in the Civil War / Traci
Nichols-Belt, with Gordon T. Belt.
p. cm.
Includes bibliographical references and index.
ISBN 978-1-60949-374-5
1. United States--History--Civil War, 1861-1865--Religious aspects. 2. Confederate States
of America. Army of Tennessee--Religion. 3. Soldiers--Religious life--United States--
History--19th century. 4. War--Religious aspects--Christianity--History--19th century. I.
Belt, Gordon T. II. Title.
E635.N58 2011
973.7'78--dc23
2011025741

For my mother, Anna Lee Nichols

Contents

Acknowledgements

This study began when I entered graduate school in the fall of 1999 working toward my master's degree in history at Middle Tennessee State University. That fall, I chose the broad topic of religion and the Civil War as the subject of my thesis. I continued my research and further defined the scope of my subject throughout my graduate studies, finishing my thesis in the spring of 2003. The body of this work was completed during those years.

The works of a number of scholars, many of whom are mentioned in the introductory chapter of this book, contributed to my understanding of this bloody conflict. They laid the foundation for my own examination into how religion influenced the lives of the soldiers who served in the Army of Tennessee, CSA. Since the completion of my research, other scholars have further reinforced my conclusion that religion played an integral role in the lives of those who fought and died in the Civil War, including Dr. George Rable, who observes in his book, *God's Almost Chosen Peoples*, "For clergy and laity alike, the war became a holy crusade."[1]

In many ways, this book has been its own crusade. My intentions from the beginning were to publish my research in an expanded form. One chapter from this book was published in the *Tennessee Historical Quarterly* in the Winter 2004 edition, but personal family obligations made it necessary for me to set this project aside for a number of years. The 2011 Sesquicentennial provided perfect motivation and timing for me to complete the work that I began so long ago. I am very grateful to The History Press and to my editor, Will McKay, for taking an interest in my book proposal and for seeing this project through to publication.

ACKNOWLEDGEMENTS

Through diaries, letters, journals, published sermons and memoirs, this book delves into the hearts and minds of the men who served in the Army of Tennessee, CSA. My husband and I owe a debt of gratitude to the institutions and archivists that provided us with access to these important records of our past, in particular John Tilford and the University Archives and Special Collections at the University of the South; Stones River National Battlefield; Taffey Hall and the Southern Baptist Historical Library and Archives; Lucinda Cockrell and the Center for Popular Music at Middle Tennessee State University; and Carol Roberts and the Tennessee State Library and Archives.

I also wish to offer my gratitude to Dr. Carroll Van West and Dr. Susan Myers-Shirk, graduate professors of history at Middle Tennessee State University, for their guidance and support. I am genuinely appreciative of their early interest in my topic and for all they have done to help make this book possible.

There are no words to adequately express my love and gratitude for my loving husband, soul mate and best friend. Gordon provided research for the illustrative material within this book and provided extensive editorial support. His advice, critique, love and prayers have also helped me beyond measure. With this project, as in our daily lives, he is a patient and dedicated partner whose support made the completion of this book possible.

Finally, I dedicate this book to the memory of my mother. From my childhood, my mother fostered within me a love for history. She initially encouraged me to pursue my graduate degree in history and later inspired my writing. My mother exemplified a godly woman whose consistent love and support I was blessed to have guide me throughout my life. She longed to see the completion of this work, and I believe somewhere in heaven she is smiling.

CHAPTER I

HISTORIOGRAPHY OF THE ROLE OF RELIGION IN THE ANTEBELLUM AND CIVIL WAR SOUTH

Do not be afraid or discouraged because of this vast army.
For the battle is not yours, but God's.
2 Chronicles 20:15 (NIV)

Wherever the Civil War raged, religion flourished. Regardless of class or position, religion permeated society, and Christian faith was the focal point of daily living. The influence of religion, especially as shaped by Confederate nationalism, on the Army of Tennessee is sparsely documented or studied, but Southern religious values clearly shaped Tennessee Confederates, contributing to both why and how they fought. *Onward Southern Soldiers* addresses this impact of religion on the members of the Army of Tennessee, CSA,[2] from its leaders to its chaplains to its common soldiers.

Religion unified the South, providing a rationalized commitment to the Confederacy. Randall Miller, Harry Stout and Charles Reagan Wilson, editors of *Religion and the American Civil War*, argued, "Politicians invoked God to justify their actions, soldiers and their families prayed for God's blessing, and religious-based organizations mobilized relief and urged reform."[3] Throughout political speeches, army orders, Sunday sermons and camp meetings, religious language and symbolism flooded Confederate communication. Religion supplied a universal language that helped to unite Southerners from various social classes, educational backgrounds and denominations to provide the Confederacy with a common purpose.

Historian Eugene Genovese suggested that Confederates, in general, envisioned themselves as a Southern David fighting a holy war against a

Northern Goliath. For several decades prior to the war, Southerners adapted religious doctrine to their distinctive cultural and social values, thereby creating a unique Southern identity with God. From this foundation emerged Southern nationalism, which was grounded in a belief that the Confederate cause was the Christian cause. Politicians, military leaders, clergy and common soldiers alike entered the war with a genuine faith in a cause they believed divine, a faith that refused any consideration for compromise with the enemy. Throughout the war, religion proved to be the Confederates' greatest weapon of warfare and the strongest builder of morale. In spite of the disparity in numbers and supplies, the faithful South began the war with an overwhelming confidence that God was on their side, and thus, victory was imminent. This foundation encouraged, motivated and comforted troops throughout the horrific trials of war.

Historians have long recognized this interplay of faith and war in the Confederacy. In 1957, James Silver espoused the view that religion was the most powerful propaganda tool used during the war. For decades, the Southern clergy had viewed Northerners as infidels. Since, in their view, God identified with the Confederacy and ordained the destiny of slavery, Southerners reasoned that the Lord would assure victory. The church sustained the people, and it preached of a divinity of slavery and the responsibility to protect both the institution of slavery and the slaves from the paganism that the clergy argued would accompany their proposed freedom. Throughout the war, the church was the major resource in building and maintaining Confederate morale. Silver concluded that Southern clergymen, as no other group, sustained the people in their long, costly and futile war for Southern independence.[4] Silver went on to argue that Southerners envisioned themselves as fighting a holy war as God's chosen people, and it was, therefore, a religious duty to fight. Southerners further regarded each victory as an answer to prayer. As the Southern cause began to deteriorate, the clergy led the nation in national days of fasting and prayer in order to repent of their sins to once again receive the favor of the Lord. The clergy passed out twenty-six million tracts promoting Southern patriotism and salvation by the fall of 1863.[5] Southerners believed the South was serving a just and stern God, but he would not abandon them, his people. The church, according to Silver, was the most powerful organization influencing the lives of men and women in the South in the days before and during the Confederacy.[6]

Herman Norton's 1961 *Rebel Religion*, in contrast, disputed the idea that religion was used for propaganda and instead focused on the sincere need

Prayer in Stonewall Jackson's Camp, etching by Adalbert J. Volck (Confederate war etchings). *Courtesy of the Library of Congress.*

of the Southern nation to have spiritual guidance during a time of horrific conflict. Norton found that the chaplainry was a major part of the framework of the military. He stated that Robert E. Lee and Thomas J. "Stonewall" Jackson adamantly supported the presence of chaplains as vital to military success. Norton envisioned the role of chaplain as one of self-denial. The chaplain was a brave and faithful companion who comforted the men and pointed the way to things that were eternal, but he also was a soldier who fought alongside the army.[7] The chaplains brought encouragement and strength in their roles as doctors, ministers and soldiers. The chaplains were also fiercely loyal to the Confederacy. Norton believed the consistent evangelism from the clergy, defeat on the battlefield and the daily facing of death created recognition of a desperate dependence on an almighty God.

A generation later, historian Sidney Romero examined religion as a weapon of warfare, combining the positions of Silver and Norton. Romero proposed that the Confederacy had a powerful weapon in religion that the North did not possess. He viewed religion as a force that molded the Confederate soldier, stating the South had a "general evangelical spirit."[8] He argued that Christianity went hand in hand with the idea of the Southern gentleman, and it also formed the justification for slavery. Religious services of all kinds were held both in the camps and on the battlefields. Soldiers heard preaching, partook of communion, engaged in prayers and attended funerals and even weddings. Before battles, it was especially important to participate in communion to once more partake of the grace of God.[9] Some soldiers risked their lives by refusing to fight on the Sabbath, and entire regiments knelt in prayer on the battlefield. Some regiments heard preaching three times a day, and soldiers spent their personal funds to purchase religious tracts. As Romero saw it, religion dispelled uncertainty, gave courage to bear trials, offered hope of a life in the hereafter and made one less fearful and, therefore, a better soldier.[10] It was the sustaining force in a soldier's endurance of years of hardship and deprivation.

Other historians have studied particular individuals, such as "Stonewall" Jackson, to demonstrate the link of religion to Confederate ideology. More recent scholars found that religion was the key to understanding Southern nationalism. Eugene Genovese proposed that the Southern armies, politicians and clergy needed and used religion to promote Southern ideals, thereby justifying their position on slavery.[11] He extensively compared the relationship of religion to the institution of slavery. Genovese argued that religious leaders viewed the struggle between North and South as a test from God to encourage His people to reform slavery to meet biblical standards. The leaders believed that without reform, the Southern nation would face the wrath of God. Their doctrine espoused that God had entrusted the South with Christian slavery, which was a necessity for the conversion of the black race. Ministers expressed the need to secure slave marriages and family life, repeal laws against slave literacy and punish cruel masters. They believed there was a proper social order, and reformed slavery was an important aspect of class structure in that order. Genovese argued, however, that Southerners enthusiastically embraced the proslavery scriptures, in part because of the prosperity that accompanied slavery. They interpreted Confederate defeats as punishment from a wrathful God for the sins of the Confederate nation. The South had failed to reform slavery. Thus, Confederates accepted the position that the Lord chastises those he loves, and "judgment begins in the House of God."[12]

In her study of Confederate nationalism, historian Drew Gilpin-Faust asserted, "The most fundamental source of legitimation for the Confederacy was Christianity."[13] It was the South's "calling" to fight for nationhood to become a peculiar people in a peculiar nation. Thus, the Southern claim to divine blessing was both a deeply held conviction and an ideological strategy designed to garner political support both abroad and at home.[14] Confederate ideology formed God into a Confederate, and thus, religious and political duty became inseparable. Southerners fused social classes and religious denominations, void of denominational rivalry, under the concept of Confederate nationalism, which was based on this unique relationship the Southerner maintained with the Almighty God. Southerners argued that God had granted the South a peculiar relationship of both blessings and responsibilities in order to enable His people to carry out their sacred charge to Christianize both the nation and what they called their "heathen race."

In order to establish a separate Christian nation and render secession and war acceptable, religion had to successfully and fervently address current issues in a manner that supported a divine Confederate cause. The clergy's ability to mold religion and the Confederacy together created a powerful foundation. Religion joined with republicanism to interpret events in the United States as part of a divine plan.[15] Theological ideas blended with cultural issues. Christine Leigh Heyrman, in *Southern Cross: The Beginnings of the Bible Belt*, followed the transition of evangelical beliefs throughout the decades preceding the Civil War to demonstrate this marriage of Southern culture and religion. A number of historians have argued that in the years prior to the war, religious leaders had to address a variety of social and cultural issues in order to ultimately promote the doctrine of a sacred Confederacy. These issues included the proper role of religion in relation to a Republican form of government, the religious aspect of slavery, the traditional role of women as religious caretakers, the masculinization of Christianity coupled with the Southern traditional concept of honor, the role of the clergy in society and government and class distinctions and class warfare.

Many members of the Southern clergy appeared to be more interested in establishing a theocracy than a separate Republican form of government. Historians Harry Stout and Christopher Grasso have argued that the Southern clergy preached the politics of secession and war and "articulated a powerful vision of the Confederacy as a chosen nation fighting a righteous crusade."[16] The clergy further published and distributed this message with great vigor and expertise. The North was viewed as a nation of infidels. To these ministers, political liberty equaled religious freedom. They espoused the claim that the United States government threatened the freedom to interpret the Bible according to one's own conscience. This was important, especially in relation to the institution of slavery. To further add to their argument, as expressed by Drew Gilpin-Faust, the clergy contended that a defensive war was always just and righteous.

FAST-DAY SERMON.

REV. I. T. TICHENOR.

"Fast Day Sermon" by Reverend Isaac Taylor Tichenor. *Courtesy of the Southern Baptist Historical Library and Archives, Nashville, Tennessee.*

The clergy used religion along with republicanism to demonstrate through United States history a God-ordained plan that dated back to Christopher Columbus. The Confederate constitution explicitly declared its Christian identity, "invoking the favor and guidance of Almighty God."[17] The national seal and motto claimed *Deo Vindice*, or "God Will Avenge." National Fast Days proclaimed by the government were a vital part of the Confederacy from its inception. The military allowed frequent religious meetings and revivals, with orders in some regiments requiring attendance. Each regiment was issued its own chaplain. The government followed the lead of the clergy and set the stage for Christian soldiers. Due to the prior decades of political and religious fusion, it was a natural transition to involve the clergy in the establishment of a new government and in the accompanying war.

Historiography of the Role of Religion in the Antebellum and Civil War South

Without a doubt, the most debated and divisive issue in the decades leading up to and during the Civil War was the institution of slavery and its place in or abolition from society. Heyrman claimed that the Southern clergy believed in the righteousness of slavery and in a sacred racial hierarchy. Genovese declared that the North charged the "Redeemer Nation" with the *sin* of slavery, thus rejecting the divine calling claimed by the South. Genovese concluded that once slavery was condemned as a sin, all proposals for gradual emancipation were rejected.[18] The North condemned the slaveholder as a wanton sinner, helping to make the war a call to holy war. The Bible was publicly revered and vital to the arguments of both regions. Both the North and the South believed their cause to be the Christian cause. The South envisioned the country as losing its soul in a search for wealth. Confederate leaders claimed that the transition from an agrarian to a market-based/industrial society had forced economic and social changes, which, in turn, led to corruption. Slaveholders claimed that the Bible blessed slavery and further impressed a sacred duty on masters to be benevolent to their slaves.[19] Christianization of what they believed was a "heathen" race became the pivotal argument in support of their peculiar institution, thereby ordaining the institution. The Southern leaders admitted the need for reforms within the institution but held to the belief that God designed the institution from the creation of the American society.

According to historian Mark Noll, nineteenth-century Americans interpreted the Bible in one of four ways with regard to slavery.[20] Some simply argued that the Bible indeed sanctioned slavery, and thus, society was required to abandon the Bible. This was the position of the most extreme among the abolitionists, such as William Lloyd Garrison and Gerrit Smith. Others argued that since the Bible sanctioned slavery, one was required to accept the institution out of loyalty to the supreme authority of God. This was the main position of Southern slave owners. Those who took the third position argued that the mere presence of slavery in the Bible was not in any way justification for the institution. Proponents insisted that the Bible had to be applied to modern life. The fourth position, which closely mirrored the third, looked to the spirit of the Bible more than to the letter of the law. Proponents moved away from the historical facts presented in the Bible and focused on the particular teachings of Jesus Christ as they related to morality. The Southern clergy were most often the victors in a literal debate of the scriptures, which convinced many in the South of the holiness of the institution. Even among those who most fervently argued the need for abolishing slavery throughout the country, a dilemma presented itself. To men like Charles Hodge of Princeton Theological Seminary, the question

Tennessee Governor Isham Green Harris was a popular two-term governor when the Civil War broke out in 1861. In response to Abraham Lincoln's call for troops to quell the Confederacy, Governor Harris replied, "Tennessee will not furnish a single man for purposes of coercion but 50,000 if necessary for the defense of our rights and those of our Southern brothers." *Courtesy of the Library of Congress.*

arose that if slavery was indeed evil, was declaring war on Christian homes the solution? Slavery was, after all, mentioned in the Bible, tolerated by the laws of the land and involved decent Christians. Was it a Christian act to declare war on sinners?[21] Most clergy struggled with these dilemmas until President Abraham Lincoln called for seventy-five thousand troops to end the rebellion, following the firing on Fort Sumter on April 12, 1861. To Southerners, the war then became a defensive war, and Confederates placed all other issues behind their absolute belief that any defensive war was just.

Throughout the war, Confederate leaders metamorphosed Christianity into a masculine image that resembled the proposed idea of the Southern Christian gentleman and soldier. Prior to the war, nineteenth-century Americans, North and South, viewed religion as the particular province of women. Women had been the primary caretakers of religion within the private domain. With religion delegated as feminine, women maintained the core responsibility of keeping the faith in the home. During the war years, according to historian James McPherson, religion left the feminine qualities of patience, meekness and resignation behind and took on the energetic, virile, masculine and muscular qualities of Christianity that were later expressed in the hymn "Onward Christian Soldiers."[22] The government, military and clergy supported this new image portraying the warrior Christian as the ideal soldier. The Christian soldier was "both Christian and Spartan, both converted and manly, and both loving and violent."[23] He resembled far more the Old Testament warrior rather than the New Testament disciple. Evangelicals like the Baptists even experienced unprecedented growth, in part due to more masculine sacraments such as immersion as opposed to sprinkling during baptism. Thousands of soldiers would line up in order to witness baptisms.[24]

This masculine image supported the idea of the sacred soldier in a sacred nation fighting a sacred cause. Religion offered the soldier distinct advantages. Faith in the hereafter diminished the fear of death and theoretically deepened the soldier's sense of duty. This belief in Providence allowed the soldier to face battles with confidence and to display courage that built the morale of his fellow comrades. Soldiers, more so than in earlier American wars, participated in revivals that swept through the army camps. In keeping with this newly created masculine ideal, the clergy gendered sins, claiming that women struggled with the sins of covetousness, pride, attachment to worldly apparel and gossip, while men most often struggled with the known camp sins of drunkenness, swearing, Sabbath breaking, gambling and, among civilian men, profiteering from the current state of affairs.[25]

Romero has argued that the new masculine ideal of Christianity supported the traditional Southern concept of honor. To the Southern gentleman, honor had always coexisted with religion. Duty to God, self and government were interrelated. Southerners believed that honor was part of the Hebraic/ Christian tradition, which was

John William Jones served as a chaplain in Robert E. Lee's Army of Northern Virginia. His reports of the ongoing revival that he had witnessed among the Confederate troops are recorded in his work, *Christ in the Camp*, published in 1887. *Courtesy of the Southern Baptist Historical Library and Archives, Nashville, Tennessee.*

rooted in scripture.[26] According to historian Bertram Wyatt-Brown, President Lincoln's call for Federal troops removed the issues of slavery, secession, politics and union and instead created the issues of self-defense, self-government and constitutional liberty, which were by their very nature bound to honor.[27] French political thinker and historian Alexis de Tocqueville noted that one of the earliest notions that came to a Southern man was that he was born to command, of ruling without resistance.[28] The Southern Christian gentleman had a duty to protect his family, home and country from invaders. This notion proposed that one was not only fighting for country but also for honor and God, and God required honor in His people. Therefore, this belief established a holy war. Each battle was thus viewed as "an act of awful and solemn worship."[29]

Within this perceived theocracy, the clergy experienced the granting to them of powerful and influential positions. According to Gilpin-Faust, the authority of the clergy rivaled that of the new Confederate state.[30] The roles delegated to the clergy throughout the war were diverse and broad-ranging. Among the activities and duties performed by the clergy during the war, one of the most vital was the nurturing and maintenance of morale. The clergy encouraged harmony among the soldiers; celebrated the government-declared days of humiliation, fasting and prayer as religious sacraments; cared for the needs of the soldiers; led in the great revivals; conducted prayer groups within the individual regiments; performed mass baptisms and weddings; and distributed religious publications. Ministers remained active throughout the war as soldiers, chaplains, officers, staff personnel and surgeons.[31] They continuously provided instruction on the proper role of the righteous leader and soldier. The clergy operated masterfully in creating comparisons between the Southern Confederacy and the

On August 21, 1863, Reverend Isaac Taylor Tichenor stood before the Alabama legislature and delivered a "Fast Day" sermon. He declared, "If God governs the world, then his hand is in this war in which we are engaged." *Courtesy of the Southern Baptist Historical Library and Archives, Nashville, Tennessee.*

children of Israel in the Old Testament. By examining the miracle victories of the Bible and comparing those to Civil War victories such as Manassas and Chancellorsville, the clergy transformed Confederate victories into supernatural miracles from an Almighty God whom they proposed clearly fought on the side of the South. Based on their position in government and politics, the clergy could assume credit when circumstances supported the theory of God conducting miracles through righteous leaders and soldiers, and they could offer explanations for battlefield defeats.

Religion further supplied the unifying force that was able to mitigate class distinctions and class warfare. Prior to the war, a great divide existed between the poor of the South and the Southern aristocracy. Throughout the war, the poor grew ever poorer, while the rich continued to host extravagant receptions flaunting their wealth.[32] Unrest from these circumstances resulted in actions like the Richmond bread riots of 1863, which could only be quelled following the arrival of the president of the Confederacy. Religion, however, was able to unite the Southern people through a perceived sacred cause. According to historian John Boles, the Confederacy was more unified religiously than it was economically or politically.[33] After all, secession to Southern Confederates was not merely a political revolution; it was a most sacred and religious charge that demanded the support of all those who claimed to be Christians.

Onward Southern Soldiers explores the centrality of religion in Confederate life with a particular focus on Tennessee Confederates, especially individual religious leaders who maintained an impact on the Army of Tennessee, CSA. This study illustrates the dissemination of the Confederate Christian message, beginning with the top of civil government and military leadership in chapter two. It then explores this message through members of the religious hierarchy, who maintained an active influence throughout the state of Tennessee. The focus then shifts to the soldiers of Tennessee, beginning with the army chaplains, who carried the Gospel message to Tennessee regiments, and finally, the recipients of the message, the common soldiers themselves, are examined. Christianity was indeed the most powerful cultural system in the Old South, and it forged a Southern identity.[34] Through primarily Tennessee voices, this study reveals how Confederate Tennesseans experienced the war as part of an army that faced cruel losses from the beginning of the war effort and, thus, an army that would have had to maintain a much greater faith in its cause than those who so often, at least in the first half of the war, experienced "miracle" battles.

Chapter 2
Political and Military Leaders

Prophetic Voices

General, he who does not see the hand of God in this is blind, sir, blind.
—*General Thomas Jonathan "Stonewall" Jackson letter to General Richard Ewell,*
June 9, 1862

Those who served in the Army of Tennessee received religious indoctrination from the highest levels of the Confederacy. Politicians and military leaders utilized religious language, symbolism and ideas to transform the civil Confederate government into a holy institution, which they claimed created the very image and embodiment of a true Christian nation. From small-town and rural ministers to the highest level of politicians, Confederate leaders used religion to support their cause, but religion proved to create far greater support for the Confederate cause than what any propagandist could have imagined.

Confederate President Jefferson Davis masterfully incorporated sacred language and symbols into the political and military realm. Prosperous Southerners such as Davis viewed the expansion and growth of the cotton kingdom as evidence that God favored Southern churches and institutions, and thus, "it reasoned that the South was the most Christian region of the nation."[35] Secession, to people like Davis, was a religious act and not merely an act of state government. In his farewell speech to the United States Senate in January 1861, Davis stated that he stood in the presence of his God. He further declared, "We will invoke the God of our fathers, who delivered them from the power of the lion, to protect us from the ravages of the bear, and thus, putting our trust in God and in our firm hearts and strong

On April 29, 1861, Jefferson Davis, president of the Confederate States of America, in his "Message on Constitutional Ratification," declared, "We feel that our cause is just and holy; we protest solemnly in the face of mankind that we desire peace at any sacrifice save that of honour and independence." *Courtesy of the Library of Congress.*

arms, we will vindicate the right."[36] Even when not discussing his personal faith, Davis incorporated Christian terminology into his speeches, thereby transporting spirituality into all secular matters. He eloquently described his abiding *faith* in the virtue and patriotism of the people; of the great *blessings* of liberty; of the *sacrifices* for *light* that were to come; of a *holy* responsibility to *sacred* institutions; and of a *sacred* duty and a movement *sanctified* by its justice that was doubly *justified* by the absence of wrong. He further explained that in his person there would be many errors to *forgive*. Davis continually invoked the blessings of Providence on a just cause, claiming that the Confederacy received a *light*, which revealed the true meaning of the Constitution written by the founding fathers.

Davis denounced what he regarded as the irreverent passion and lust of dominion that had clouded the judgment and inflamed the ambition of the United States. He asserted that the Confederacy "must prepare to meet the emergency and to maintain, by the final arbitrament of the sword, the position which we have assumed among the nations of the earth."[37] "Obstacles may retard," he observed, but "they cannot long prevent the progress of a movement sanctified by its justice, and sustained by a virtuous people."[38] His justification for secession and war was founded in his belief that "He who knows the hearts of men will judge of the sincerity with which we labored to preserve the government of our fathers in its spirit."[39] He prayed: "Reverently let us invoke the God of our fathers to guide and protect us in our efforts to perpetuate the principles which, by His blessing, they were able to vindicate, establish, and transmit to their posterity, and with a continuance of His favor, ever gratefully acknowledged, we may hopefully look forward to success, to peace, and to prosperity."[40]

At Richmond, Virginia, in June 1861, Davis maintained that God had devolved a "high and holy responsibility" on the Confederacy, entrusting them to preserve the constitutional liberty of a free government. He further argued:

> *Those with whom we have lately associated have shown themselves so incapable of appreciating the blessings of the glorious institutions they inherited, that they are today stripped of the liberty to which they were born. They have allowed an ignorant usurper to trample upon all the prerogatives of citizenship, and to exercise power never delegated to him; and it has been reserved for your own State, so lately one of the original thirteen, but now, thank God, fully separated from them, to become the theatre of a great central camp, from which will pour forth thousands of brave hearts to roll back the tide of this despotism. Apart from that gratification we may well feel at being separated from such a connection, is the pride that upon you devolves the task of maintaining and defending our new government. I believe that we shall be able to achieve the noble work, and that the institutions of our fathers will go to our children as sacred as they have descended to us.*[41]

Davis admitted that Confederates would indeed encounter awesome sacrifices in carrying forward the sacred charge placed upon the South, but he contended that "under the smiles of the God of the just," Confederates would be endowed with the spirit of the founding fathers and would achieve a great and conclusive success. He prayed with the hope that all within the Confederacy would pray to God to crown the Confederate cause and country with success and victory.

Some of the most passionate pleas for the heralded sacred cause were voiced at the frequent days of humiliation, fasting and prayer in both the South and North. Davis called for a universal observance of fasting on nine separate occasions.[42] President Abraham Lincoln proclaimed three days of fasting and prayer.[43] Individual states, legislators and church bodies organized many other similar days. On fasting days, the government encouraged citizens to pray morning, noon and night and to reside in humiliation of body, mind and spirit. The theme of the fast days followed the example of the fast proclaimed in the Bible by the prophet Ezra, who expressed that "the hand of our God is upon all them for good that seek Him."[44] During the days of prayer and fasting, Confederates lifted pleas for the Almighty to once again shine the light of His countenance upon the Southern armies and bless them while simultaneously confounding the enemy and delivering them into the hands of the South. Confederates acknowledged their weakness, but they rejoiced that in their weakness, God was made strong. Thus, victories became "miracles" that were compared with those of the Israelites at the Red Sea.

The same level of religious fervor found among Confederate officials such as Jefferson Davis could also be found among leading army commanders. General Robert E. Lee embodied the idea of the Christian Confederate. Although a professional soldier, he was viewed as a lover of people, including Northerners, and a devout Christian. On April 25, 1861, Lee wrote, "No earthly act would give me so much pleasure as to restore peace to my country, but I fear it is now out of the power of man, and in God alone must be our trust."[45] Lee, along with General "Stonewall" Jackson, strongly supported the presence of chaplains in the Confederate army. In 1861, Lee issued orders requiring all noncommissioned officers and privates to attend religious services, and commissioned officers were expected to attend of their own accord.[46] Many historians have proposed that Lee genuinely believed he was doing God's will and that God was watching out for him and for his cause.[47] Throughout the horrific trials of war, his personal walk with God and his faith deepened. As defeat and ruin grew nearer, many Confederates, like Lee, recognized a greater dependence on God and grew nearer to Him, as evidenced by the great revivals that began in 1863. Although Lee is primarily remembered for his great military capabilities, he is further remembered for his pious daily walk with God.

In a letter to his wife on Christmas Day 1862, two weeks after the Battle of Fredericksburg, General Robert E. Lee wrote, "I pray that, on this day when only peace and good-will are preached to mankind, better thoughts may fill the hearts of our enemies and turn them to peace." *Courtesy of the Library of Congress.*

An even better example of a Confederate general who envisioned himself as carrying out God's will was General Thomas Jonathan "Stonewall" Jackson. According to historian James I. Robertson Jr., Jackson ranks among the six greatest soldiers that America has ever produced, and his death was the greatest personal loss suffered by the Confederates and one that permanently crippled the wartime South.[48] Jackson was known for his stubborn determination to overcome hardships and for his deep religious faith and convictions. Prior to the war, Jackson had served as a Presbyterian deacon and Sunday school teacher in Lexington, Virginia, while employed as a professor at the Virginia Military Institute (VMI). During the Civil War, General Richard Taylor wrote of Jackson, "Praying and fighting appeared to be his idea of the whole duty of man."[49] At the time of his death, his devotion to God was as greatly known as his ability on the battlefield.

Major General F.H. Smith of the VMI wrote of Jackson following his death, "He was an example of all that is good and great and true in the character of a Christian Soldier. He became a soldier of the Cross and as a humble conscientious and useful Christian man he established the character which has developed into the world renowned Christian Hero."[50] Smith further announced to the cadets at the VMI that Jackson was emphatically a man of God and that his faith impressed every act of his life. Prior to the war, Jackson refused to read a newspaper, write a letter or discuss secular subjects on a Sunday.[51] Prior to and during the war, Jackson began every task by first seeking the blessing of God, and he finished his tasks by offering thanks to God.

Jackson himself expressed similar sentiments as those offered as a memorial to him years earlier in a letter to his sister, Laura, following the death of Jackson's first wife, Eleanor. "She has now gone on a glorious visit though through a gloomy portal," he remarked. "Her companions are of the glorified Host. I look forward with delight to the day when I shall join her. Religion is all that I desire it to be. I am reconciled to my loss and have joy in a future reunion where the wicked cease from troubling and the weary are at rest."[52] To the Confederate South, Jackson symbolized the bold and

General Thomas Jonathan "Stonewall" Jackson's devotion to God was as greatly known as his ability on the battlefield, and his faith guided his thought and character. *Courtesy of the Library of Congress.*

fearless soldier whose courage came from a complete confidence in God and knowledge of a glorious hereafter.

Jackson believed God favored Confederate nationalism, and so, the war was a holy crusade. He proposed that the North had violated principles set in place by the founding fathers and Christ. God had chosen the road that America was to take, and to alter American structure would be to alter the plan of God.[53] His staff was composed of devout Christians with the same ideology.[54]

Jackson claimed that victories came solely from God, and success was to be sought in the name of God. In June 1862, following a Union retreat after the Battle of Port Republic, Jackson exclaimed to General Richard Ewell, "General, he who does not see the hand of God in this is blind, sir, blind."[55] Jackson had started out the day by acknowledging the blessings of God on his army on the previous day and seeking God's protection and blessing for an even greater success on this day.

Jackson was known to even administer himself the rite of communion prior to battle. He envisioned himself as a military instrument used of God in a holy war. Jackson believed that God had ordained the Civil War to sanctify the land. He prayed fervently and frequently with the sincere belief that with God's help, nothing was impossible.[56] It would be impossible to adequately portray the military life of Jackson while ignoring the religious element. A captain who had served under Jackson wrote thirty years following the conclusion of the war, "Jackson's fame was as lasting as the solid stone of his native hills, and yet there was for him a purer, nobler record—his quiet Christian walk in life, his right words, his faithful, manly bearing, his victory over self, his known devotion to the word of truth. He was indeed a soldier of the cross."[57] Jackson's religious positions directed his stand on secession and the war from the outset.

The wartime correspondence of Jackson, whether intended for family, friends or military personnel, and the correspondence regarding Jackson were flooded with references to God and requests for prayer for military success. On July 31, 1862, Jackson wrote his friend Dr. Francis McFarland, thanking him for his prayers for the success of operations and troops that God had entrusted to Jackson. Jackson stated:

> *I am very grateful to you for your prayers to God for the success of the operation, which God has entrusted to me. Please continue to pray for me and for the success of the troops entrusted to me. It cheers my heart to think that many of God's people are praying to our very kind Heavenly Father for the success of the army to which I belong. Without God's blessing I look for*

no success, and for every success my prayer is, that all the glory may be given unto Him to whom it is properly due. If people would but give all the glory to God, and regard his creatures as but unworthy instruments, my heart would rejoice. Alas too frequently the praise is bestowed upon the creature. Whilst we must not forget the superior importance of spiritual victories, yet I trust that you will under God's direction do what you can in securing the prayers of His people for the success of our arms, especially for the success of them which are entrusted to me, an unworthy servant, but who desires to glorify His name even in my present military calling. My trust is in God for success.[58]

Many Confederate soldiers envisioned Jackson as the true Southern Christian hero, accepting his death as the calling of God. Soldier Abram Fulkerson told his wife: "I always had great reverence for the man on account of his piety and uprightness of character. Among the many heroes of this revolution, none have lived so much adored, none have died so much

In this image, General Thomas Jonathan "Stonewall" Jackson is memorialized in bronze and stone at his grave site in Lexington, Virginia. *Author's collection.*

deplored, and none have left a character as spotless as that of Stonewall Jackson. God has seen proper to take him from us, and what He does is right and for the best."[59] General Lee also proposed that the death of Jackson was the will of God, but in return, he expected God to raise up another "Stonewall." Major General F.H. Smith comforted the VMI cadets following Jackson's death. He observed, "God gave him to us, and to his country. He fitted him for his work, and when his work was done He called him to Himself. Submissive to the will of his Heavenly Father, it may be said of him, that while in every heart there may be some murmuring, his will was to do and suffer the will of God."[60]

The Confederate clergy, in a perplexed state following Jackson's death, developed a biblical theory explaining both his unexpected death and his relation to the divine call of the Confederacy. Ministers explained that just as God had used Moses to lead his children into liberty but had refused to allow Moses, His divine instrument, to accompany the Israelites into the Promised Land and their destiny, God had likewise chosen his servant Jackson to be a leader in delivering His servant the South into its liberty. God also had chosen to prevent Jackson from seeing the completion of the promise but had instead called him home to his reward in Heaven, leaving another to complete the victory.[61] Even the fact that Jackson died as the result of a stray bullet from his own men, and did not succumb until the Sunday following his wounding, spoke to the hand of Providence being involved in the action.[62]

Other members of the clergy, such as Reverend R.F. Bunting, chaplain to the Eighth Texas Cavalry in the Army of Tennessee, believed that Jackson's death came as a divine chastisement of God for the idolization that the Confederate people maintained for the military commander. The clergy actively published and distributed sermons relating to and explaining Jackson's death throughout the Confederacy. Regardless of the degree of acceptance given to the various explanations of Jackson's death, many soldiers throughout the Confederacy recognized, respected and followed the Christian example displayed through this "soldier of the cross." Historian James Robertson Jr. declared, "Stonewall Jackson more than anyone else personified the compelling and the virtuous in what subsequent generations would label The Lost Cause."[63]

An example of an Army of Tennessee general who commingled religion with the Confederate cause was General Leonidas Polk. The Episcopal bishop of Louisiana, Polk left the pulpit and donned the gray in his support for the Confederate cause. Polk, a graduate of West Point, resigned his commission following graduation in order to study for the ministry, entering

The Right Reverend (General)
Leonidas Polk, CSA, seen here in
his bishop's uniform, was among
the founders of the University of
the South in Sewanee, Tennessee.
Courtesy of the Library of Congress.

The Right Reverend (General)
Leonidas Polk, CSA. *Courtesy of
the University Archives and Special
Collections, The University of the South.*

Theological Seminary at Alexandria, Virginia. At an early age, Polk's family had immigrated to Tennessee. In 1830, Polk was ordained a deacon, and in 1833, he made his residence in Maury County, Tennessee. While living in Maury County, Polk assumed charge of the Columbia parish and aided Bishop James H. Otey in establishing the Columbia Institute for Women, which opened in 1834. Polk further, with the aid of his brothers, erected St. John's Episcopal Church in Maury County, Tennessee. In 1836, Polk was ordained as an Episcopal priest. In 1841, he assumed the duties as the bishop for the Southwest and of the Diocese of Louisiana, which he held for twenty years prior to his service in the Confederate army. Polk was also among the founders of the University of the South in Sewanee, Tennessee, in 1857.

Stephen Elliott—bishop of the Diocese of Georgia, co-founder of The University of the South at Sewanee and, following the death of James Otey, bishop of the Confederacy—described Polk as leaving the possibilities of an illustrious military career behind him in order to instead become a "soldier of the Cross." Once the Civil War commenced, however, Polk transformed his life once again. Polk, a close friend of President Davis, was appointed a major general in the Provisional Army of the Confederacy in June 1861 and later, in 1862, was promoted to lieutenant general.[64] "The Fighting Bishop," as Polk was known, held command over the defense of the Mississippi Valley and commanded forces from Shiloh to Chickamauga. He was killed while on reconnaissance at Pine Mountain on June 14, 1864. During the war, Polk baptized Generals Joseph E. Johnston and John Bell Hood. Thus, Polk retained certain priestly responsibilities, which he coupled with his military duties as general.

Polk, a plantation owner and a slave trader and owner, proposed that the United States army's "irruption and invading would be the advent of all disorder and irreligion into his state and Diocese."[65] At the beginning of his military service, the general consensus of the Episcopal clergy was against his leaving the church to engage in battle, but he maintained supporters from the highest ranks of the church. Bishop Elliott wrote, "Very little was said at the convention, in my presence at least, upon the subject of your acceptance of military office. The general feeling was against it among the clergy, but Mr. Pollard, whose opinion I know you value, was very glad of it. My opinion coincided very much with that of Bishop Meade, that, as a general thing, it was inexpedient, but in your particular case and under the circumstances very defensible."[66] Polk attempted to later resign his army commission, but the clergy assured him of their approval, and they cited Old Testament examples to justify Polk's "taking up the sword," which he had earlier laid down at the feet of Christ when he resigned his commission following graduation from West Point.[67]

From the onset of his military assignment, Polk gazed toward heaven to receive direction in battle, answers to defeats and hope for a lasting and final victory for the Confederacy. Polk brazenly carried his faith into battle and displayed his faith and convictions continuously before his men. In a letter to his wife, Polk stated, "Our trust is in the living God, to whom we look for wisdom to guide us and courage to sustain us; and may He be with us ever more!"[68] Upon accepting the position over the department of the Southwest, Polk issued General Orders No. 1 from his headquarters in Meridian, Mississippi, on December 23, 1863. He thus proclaimed to the troops now under his command:

In taking charge of the Department, the Lieut. General commanding is not insensible of the importance of the duties devolved upon him, or the difficulties by which he is surrounded. The extent of the territory embraced in the command, its geographical position, its sea ports, its river coast, its resources in men and material—still untouched and available—constitute it a field of the highest importance to the Confederacy in its military aspects. Its difficulties and embarrassments, whatever they may be, are not inherent, nor are they insurmountable. Chargeable mainly to the fortunes of war, they are to be regarded as trials of our fidelity to the cause we have espoused, and tests of the sincerity, and depth, and earnestness of our devotion to its final triumph. Reverses as well as successes are the allotments of war. Let us hope that the future may be more generous to us than the past. And when we consider the high soldierly qualities of the army belonging to this command, and call to mind the lofty traits of character which have ever distinguished the populations comprised within its limits, we cannot but feel that the time has come when for us there is to be a more favorable turn of the wheel of fortune. We may, nevertheless, remember that it was a maxim of the religion of the heathen that the gods helped those who helped themselves, a maxim which the teachings of a purer and truer faith have served to confirm and establish. Our cause is not less the cause of truth, of honor, and of God, now, than it was the day we first took up arms against the barbarous horde of fanatics and of Puritan and German infidels who have for three years sought to despoil us of our political rights, rob us of our property, destroy our social life, and overturn and crush our altars. The hate of these men has not been abated by the plunder and desolation and bloodshed upon which it has fed, but rather been deepened and intensified. From them, should they succeed, we are to expect nothing but universal confiscation of our property, abject social and personal degradation or death. The Lieut. General commanding, therefore, confidently trusts that under a sense of such a hopeless future, the inspiration of our just cause, and the encouragement and example of our noble women, who everywhere regard our invaders with loathing and abhorrence, all past grievances among ourselves, real or supposed, may be forgotten; and while the gallant men who compose our army in the field will resolve afresh to renew their vows of undying resistance to our enemy, those who have not yet taken up arms will come forward, promptly, to swell the ranks of our battalions, and share with their countrymen the duty and honor of breaking the power of the oppressor. The vigorous employment of our own resources, with unity, harmony, and an unflinching determination to be free, cannot, under God, but crown our efforts with triumphant success.[69]

Polk's letters to his family, as well as those written to military personnel and soldiers, expressed his belief that he was waging war in a righteous campaign. On June 1, 1864, in a letter to his daughter Lilly, only days prior to his death on the field, Polk wrote, "Our army is in good spirits and confident, under the blessing of God, of success in the coming conflict. It is also in high condition. Our trust is in God. May the good Lord bless and keep you and yours, my dear child, in all your coming experiences and trial of life, and afterward receive you to glory, is the prayer of your affectionate father."[70]

A portrait of Confederate General Joseph E. Johnston. *Courtesy of the Library of Congress.*

Following the death of General Polk, General Joseph E. Johnston wrote of him on June 14, 1864, "In this distinguished leader we have lost the most courteous of gentlemen, the most gallant of soldiers. The Christian, patriot, soldier, has

Balm for the Weary and Wounded by Charles Todd Quintard. *Courtesy of the University Archives and Special Collections, The University of the South.*

neither lived nor died in vain. His example is before you—his mantle rests with you."[71] Bishop Elliott, alluding to this example of the righteous soldier sacrificed for the Confederate army, proclaimed during Polk's funeral service that Polk's final act had been one of prayer, contemplation and communion with his God. To Elliott, this explained why Polk had lingered on the bluff while other generals—Joseph E. Johnston, William Hardee and W.H. Jackson—had scattered once the first shell was directed at them. Elliott further described Polk's torn body as being found with his face upturned, his broken arms crossed upon his breast and his prayerful expression lingering upon his face. In Polk's pockets, stained with his blood, were found his *Book of Common Prayer* and four copies of a manual entitled *Balm for the Weary and Wounded.*

In Elliott's funeral address for Polk, the bishop vehemently declared the righteousness of the cause for which Polk sacrificed his life. He continuously compared the martyrs of the Bible with those who were fallen on the field of battle for the "glorious" South. The bishop proclaimed:

In the history of the Church of Christ the death of its most illustrious saints has taken the revolting form of violence. Some have gone to glory imitating Christ in the shame and agony of the Cross. Others have ascended to the gates of Paradise in chariots of fire. The spirit of the Martyr Stephen passed away amid the curses of an infuriated mob; and the gentle James was smitten with the sword of ruthless tyranny. Why, then, stand appalled that, in these latter days our brother should have died by the hand of violence? Has human nature changed? Has fanaticism learned any mercy? We have been plainly told in Holy Writ that, in the latter days, perilous times should come, and come they have to us. Do ye not hear the voices of your own brethren, Ministers and Bishops, hounding on these hordes of lawless men to the desolation of our homes, our altars, our families, ourselves? The body which lies before us is the last, but not the only one, of our martyred Bishops. The heart of the gentle, loving Cobbs was broken by the vision of coming evil which he foresaw. The lion-hearted Meade died just when the hand of destruction was laid upon his quiet home, and its sacred associations were scattered to the winds. Otey, the high-souled, the honest-hearted, the guileless, expired a prisoner in his own home, his closing eyes looking upon a desolated diocese, a scattered and ruined people, and exiled ministry—all the work of his life in ruins. The mangled corpse of our beloved brother closes, for the present, the succession of our Episcopal martyrs. Who shall come next? I, in the proper order of succession. God's will be done. My only prayer is, that, if He sees necessary, I may die in defense of the same holy cause, and with the like faith and courage. Our brother fills the grave of a Christian warrior! Although a minister of the Prince of Peace and a Bishop in the Church of God, he has poured out his life-blood for us upon the field of battle.[72]

Elliott compared Polk's joining the army to that of the Lord's cleansing of the Temple, where He lashed out violently, as a man of war, at those dishonoring His Father's house. He stated that Polk waged war clothed in the full armor of God, albeit in a different sense than one typically related to a minister of the Church of Christ. Men wielded different weapons indeed, but Elliott argued that these, nonetheless, were equally spiritual when conducting a battle waged for the sake of righteousness. Soldiers had to meet and challenge their enemy with the armament of God in the same manner that their enemy met and challenged them. Elliott claimed that this was not only right but also glorious in the sight of God. Elliott eloquently recalled various instances from the Bible in which, "mingled with the grace and the love of the Gospel, a spirit of fiery indignation" rose and swelled in the hearts and souls of the apostles, martyrs, saints and even the Lord himself.[73] He claimed it was this same fiery indignation and calling that had "elected, called, prepared, and placed" Polk in the action of the war. This was a calling that overpowered any attempt for resistance but caused one instead to submit himself as a "mere instrument in God's hands, doing His will, driven by His spirit, supported by His strength, and dying as His martyr."[74] Elliott believed it was a wonderful coincidence that the one who abandoned his sword to the services of the Lord so young in his life would in his old age pick up that sword to resume to fight the battles of religion and the church. Elliott claimed that Polk had laid down his duties as a bishop comparatively as Christ had abandoned his glory to come to earth, and he further stated that on the Sunday preceding his death, Polk had partaken of communion, thus anointing himself for his burial, again creating an association between Polk and Jesus Christ. Elliott ended his funeral address by stating:

> *It is a very striking fact that every officer of high rank in that army—the army which, in the language of General Johnston, he created, and had always commanded—has become a professed disciple of the meek and lowly Jesus; and that the last act of our warrior-bishop was the admission into the Church of his Saviour and Redeemer, through the holy sacrament of baptism, of two of its most renowned commanders. He lived long enough to see Christ recognized in its councils of war; and, his work on earth being done, he obeyed the summons of his master, and passing away from earth, his mantle rests upon it.*[75]

Elliott connected Polk's experiences and accomplishments with the common thread of faith. Elliott stated:

> *Whatever Christian work he took in hand, he labored at it with all his heart and soul. His early missionary work, his later diocesan supervision, his interest in the advancement of the slave, his grand university scheme, his military career, were all marked by a like intense devotion and absorption. During his conception and conduct of that glorious scheme of education, which will remain as his enduring monument, I was his chosen colleague and constant companion.*[76]

Although Elliott proposed that The University of the South at Sewanee, Tennessee would stand as Polk's crowning achievement, he nonetheless viewed Polk's military actions as having been equally critical in forwarding the cause of Christ.

Civilians responded to this call of holy war by enthusiastically supporting their leaders in the "Christian" cause whom they sincerely viewed as righteous. Sarah Dorsey, a wealthy plantation mistress from Louisiana, mailed a letter to Polk on February 20, 1862, which accompanied a Christian banner adorned with the Cross of Constantine that she had specifically created for his army. In the letter she stated, "Recognizing the holiness of our cause, I have feared to use the sacred Christian symbol especially as I designed to put in the hands of a Christian apostle. Believing as I do that we are fighting the Battle of the Cross, against the Modern Barbarians who would rob a Christian people of Country, Liberty, and Life. As long as I live my prayers go up continually to the King of Kings, that He may protect and deliver us from the hands of the strong and deadly set against us."[77] Following the death of General Polk, as the funeral procession passed through the streets of Augusta, Georgia, where all places of business had been closed, houses, balconies and walkways were crowded with an assembly of civilians who came out to pay their respects of loving tribute to their departed Soldier of the Cross.

Christianity formed the foundation as well as the legitimation for the Civil War. Religion provided the language, the symbols and the charismatic speakers to debate and promote Southern nationalism. This nationalism converted God into a Confederate. One's duty to God and to nation was one and the same. Ministers, politicians and soldiers alike drew from American constitutionalism and conservative Christianity to create a Confederate identity. The South was characterized as being inherently superior in righteousness compared to the North and, thus, invincible.

The Christian religious beliefs of President Davis and many of his military commanders formed from the roots of a genuine and sincere faith that was an integral part of Southern life. As historian Edward L. Ayers observed, "It was the Confederacy and not its enemy who inscribed 'Almighty God' into its Constitution and who raised 'God Will Avenge' as its motto. Davis frequently invoked the Christian God even as Abraham Lincoln spoke in more mystical religious language. The Confederacy considered itself the first great Christian nation, the instrument of God's will, the beginning of something rather than its end."[78] Devotion, perseverance and passion grounded in the Christian faith were the heart and soul of the Confederacy, and the religious examples of eloquent, talented and brave leaders such as Davis, Lee, Jackson and Polk transfused a purpose and foundation into the newly established Confederacy that formed an extraordinary pride and determination. Together, these imbued a spirit of invincibility in the Confederate heart that assured Confederate soldiers of an absolute impending victory.

CHAPTER 3

ELITE SOUTHERN MINISTERS

Apostles for "Working Out God's Purposes"

The race is not to the swift, nor the battle to the strong, but our trust is in the name of the Lord our God.
—*Bishop Stephen Elliott, February 28, 1862*

In an age when people lived for far fewer years than today, Southerners, like most Americans, lived in anticipation of death and the hereafter. Many Southerners recognized the presence of God in every event, thus establishing the church as the central force around which all else in their lives revolved. The church existed not only as a center for spiritual needs but also as a forum for political action, an avenue for education and an arena for socializing. Due to the prominence of the church, the clergy maintained a high degree of influence and control over society, a cultural hegemony that rivaled even the authority of the leaders of the Confederacy during the Civil War. From this position of power, ministers within the Confederacy heralded a war cry for Southern independence, grounded in Christian faith and principles, which paved the road to secession and war.

Prior to the Civil War, religious leaders articulated a clear connection between church doctrine and the affairs of the state. This seemingly sacred relationship told of a Confederate peculiar identity with God, the destiny and history of slavery and the presence of the Lord in victory and in defeat. The churches had experienced a division several years prior to the division of the nation, a foreshadowing of what was to come. The Baptists, Methodists and Presbyterians all split from their Northern brethren prior to the Civil War.

The Episcopal Church, although not formally splitting, created a separate association for the South following secession.

Ministers utilized sermons, tracts and religious newspapers in order to promote a rebellion against tyranny and injustice for the proposed purpose of securing religious freedom. A flood of religious writings inundated the Confederate army, and soldiers used their hard-earned cash to purchase tracts.[79] "Although originally only a religious paper, the *South Western Baptist* came during the war to have such political influence as to be suppressed by Union authorities after the defeat of the Confederacy," asserted historian Malcolm C. McMillan.[80] The newspapers contained fiery speech designed to fan into flames the passions of the soldiers. One article for the *South Western Baptist* stated, "In the name of our God, we will set up our banners; and by the blessings of Him who ruleth in the armies of heaven, the sword will never be sheathed until the last invader shall be driven from our shores. Let prayer be made without ceasing unto God, and the result is not doubtful."[81]

Scholars Randall Miller, Harry Stout and Charles Reagan Wilson, in *Religion and the American Civil War*, argue that "Bible, tract, home missionary, and Sunday school societies, along with hundreds of religious newspapers, provided common reading materials that reached across a vast continent as religious leaders tried to create a Christian American empire. Advice books and magazines, even popular fiction, purveyed religious themes."[82] According to Kurt O. Berends, the religious military press played a dynamic role in evangelizing soldiers, articulating war aims and building morale. The editors of the religious military press and members of the clergy identified the Confederacy as holy from the beginning and thereby blurred any distinctions between secular and sacred in their nurturing of a Southern civil religious patriotism.[83] Mark A. Noll discovered:

> *Up to and through the Civil War, publishing and distribution of the Bible dwarfed all other American enterprises relating to books. During the war itself, the American Bible Society distributed more than three million Bibles and New Testaments to combatants; something like 300,000 Bibles passed from northern publishers into the South (despite a ban on trade between the sections); and Moses Hoge of Richmond by himself braved the Union blockade to smuggle 10,000 Bibles, 50,000 New Testaments, and 250,000 portions of Psalms and Gospels from England back to the South.*[84]

As the religious military press distributed thousands of newspapers within the South, they turned the camp revivals into major cultural events. The revivals, they believed, illustrated that God must be with their army and their cause, as evidenced by the outpouring of His grace and power. The *Soldier's Paper*, in an article entitled "The Revival in the Army of Tennessee," made the claim that "50 to 100 join the church daily in the Army of Tennessee."[85]

Elite ministers also added their voices to this inundation of religious material through the publication of sermons often prepared and preached specifically to rally soldiers for the Southern cause. Political leaders often requested that ministers publish specific sermons for distribution to the Confederate army. Following the national days of humiliation, fasting and prayer, elite ministers would regularly receive requests for their sermons so that distribution could be made, often in tract form, to the soldiers.

Most of the Confederate clergy reinforced, or even extended, the official message that God was on the side of the Confederacy in the Civil War. Confederates envisioned themselves as the "chosen people" who had remained faithful to their God while the North had forsaken the truths of the gospel in order to worship their new God of greed. Many Confederates viewed themselves as the godliest of all people who alone held a claim to divine blessing. They believed that God had anointed the Confederacy with both a special status and special responsibilities, and so, for each benefit there existed an obligation.[86]

The Episcopal Church primarily represented the Southern planter aristocracy, which instigated much of the divisiveness between the regions at the time prior to and during the Civil War. This denomination, along with the evangelical denominations, became a source of powerful and consistent voices for Southern nationalism, the doctrine of divine slavery and general war propaganda. Bishop James H. Otey—bishop of the Diocese of Tennessee and senior bishop of the Confederacy—and Bishop Stephen Elliott—bishop of the Diocese of Georgia and the presiding bishop of the Protestant Episcopal Church in the Confederate States of America—joined with evangelical voices including that of John Lansing Burrows, pastor of the First Baptist Church in Richmond, who specifically directed sermons to Tennessee soldiers concerning Tennessee events. These were all prominent bishops and ministers serving in the Confederate states. Many ministers who remained behind the lines of fire in the somewhat safer locations of the pulpit published sermons that addressed the battles occurring and the soldiers fighting in the Army of Tennessee that were distributed for purposes of comfort and morale. As each bishop and minister struggled with the issues of the troubled times, each developed distinct and personal answers to the questions that were raised by the war.

The Episcopal bishop of Texas, Alexander Gregg, spoke for many Confederate ministers when he alerted his brethren, "Never before in our history has such an opportunity been afforded for the Church to appear in her true relations to the State."[87] Following secession, the church almost immediately began a tenacious attack on the Union in its uncompromising support of its new nation. The clergy claimed the Confederacy stood on more solid ideological and practical ground than the American revolutionaries had in their "rebellion." The revolutionary fathers had declared themselves independent from their mother country while they were merely colonies, which had a degree of rebellion to it. The actions of the colonies could not compare with sovereign states declaring and reclaiming once again their sovereignty. If the founding fathers were just in their actions, it was argued that the South could not be unjust in theirs. If the South were in a state of rebellion or insurrection, the circumstances would be different, but as Bishop Elliott claimed, they were not in any such condition, for this was a revolution. Elliott stated, "The State, in the exercise of her unquestioned sovereignty resumed the powers which she had delegated to the Federal Government,

The Right Reverend James Hervey Otey. *Courtesy of the University Archives and Special Collections, The University of the South.*

and confederated herself with the other states forming an entirely new government under a constitution prepared with great wisdom, moderation, and with fasting and prayer."[88] Explaining that constitutional avenues had been exhausted, ministers employed every tactic and method at their disposal to promote their righteous revolution.

Tennessee Bishop James Hervey Otey was chosen by the Confederate States of America to serve as a leader in the "second American revolution." The Episcopal Church elected Otey first bishop of Tennessee in 1833. In 1836, Otey founded the Columbia Institute in Columbia, Tennessee, and in 1841, as bishop of Tennessee, he was granted jurisdiction over Florida, Mississippi, Arkansas and the Indian Territory. On July 4, 1857, he was named first chancellor of the University of the South. Illness prevented Otey's attendance at the preliminary council of the Southern Diocese in Montgomery, Alabama, in July 1861, but he was present the following October in Columbia, South Carolina, at the organization of the Protestant Episcopal Church in the Confederate States of America. Upon the death of Bishop Meade of Virginia, Otey became senior bishop of the church in the Confederate States of America, a position he held only a short time.[89] Bishop Otey died in Memphis on April 23, 1863.

Prior to the outbreak of the Civil War, Otey opposed the position of his colleagues, Bishop Elliott and Bishop Leonidas Polk, remaining emphatically pro-Union. In 1857, in a statement concerning the chosen name of "Southern University," which Northerners regarded as a sign of sectionalism, Otey explained:

> We affirm that our aim is eminently national and patriotic, and as such, should commend itself to every lover of his country. I repel the suspicion to which imaginary fears have given birth. Will the sons of those who fought and bled in the cause of liberty, lift a voice or hand against the union of these states? There are some of us here today, in whose veins flows the blood of men who fought in almost every battle, from Saratoga to the disastrous repulse at Savannah, and to the crowning victory at Yorktown. And when we shall be found, under color or religion, hatching treason against the peace and union of these states, may desolation roll its wave over our habitations, and our names be swallowed up in infamy![90]

Bishop Otey, writing to his friends Bishops Elliott and Polk, strongly and consistently urged allegiance to the Union. Otey, however, finally and reluctantly accepted secession as inevitable following a final attempt to avert war by forwarding a letter to Secretary of State William Seward, in which he assured the secretary that the South was not contemplating any attack on the North and in which he beseeched the secretary to prevent any attack on the South.

Otey recognized, as did Elliott and Polk, the religious nature of society as a whole. Otey contended:

> The religious interests of the country are inseparable from the social and the civil. Christianity—not any particular form of its expression, but the

religion of Christ, as exemplified in the lives of himself and Apostles—is rooted beneath our platforms of government, and ramified throughout our civil and social institutions so widely and so strongly that the one cannot be plucked up without ruining the other. The religion of Christ is at the bottom of the whole.[91]

With this recognition of the integral workings combining the political, social and religious elements of society, the path was made ready for Otey's Confederate transformation.

Once war commenced, Otey defended the Southern Confederate cause with great enthusiasm and vigor. In a pastoral letter written in 1861, he wrote:

Let no man's heart fail him because of the railings and threats that are made against us. Under the lead of a fanaticism which stoops to the use of appeals to the worst passions of human nature—which, in the ardor of its zeal to accomplish its purposes, sets aside the fear of God, and actually rejects and denies the authority of His Holy Word, a very large portion of the people of the Northern States have been roused to make war upon us, and armies are gathering on our borders for the avowed object of carrying fire and sword, ruin and desolation, from the banks of the Ohio to the Gulf of Mexico. Possessed with an unaccountable infatuation, they allege, in justification of their course, grievances of whose existence we are unconscious, and pretend an apprehension of invasion of their territory, and assault upon their rights, which we have not even meditated.[92]

Otey also complained about forty years of Northern aggression, during which the Northern people ignored the laws of the government in order to oppose the South and Southern institutions. He argued it was natural for alienation to occur between the sections of the nation due to this unfair treatment given the South. Otey compared the Federal mobilization in spring 1861 with the earlier events at Harpers Ferry, Virginia. The bishop pronounced, "Notwithstanding all the past, there were hundreds of thousands in the South, who, in their love of, and devotion to the Federal Union, were willing to bear more, until the proclamation of President Lincoln, inaugurating war, had destroyed the last germ of hope that we could reach a peaceful solution of our difficulties."[93] He emphasized that the South was fighting a defensive war against aggression and that there were no plans of aggression on the part of Southern armies. Otey quoted the Psalmist by writing, "We are for peace, but when we speak thereof, they make them ready to battle."[94] He, therefore, encouraged his colleagues and parishioners alike by writing:

> We have, therefore, no alternative, but to meet force with force and repel aggression as best we may, and commit our cause to Him that judgeth righteously. Let us all do our whole duty faithfully, as Christians and citizens, and we need not fear what man can do unto us, "The battle is not always to the strong." "The Lord shall give strength unto his people: the Lord shall give His people the blessing of peace." While, then, we pray for our sons and brethren who have gone forth to breast the storm of battle for the cause of our people and our God, let us not forget that our sins have brought upon us all the evils that now threaten us. Let us make haste to confess our sins, to repent us truly of our faults, ask God's merciful pardon and forgiveness through Christ, so "iniquity shall not be our ruin." And while doing this for ourselves, let us not forget that Christ died for his and our enemies, as well as for ourselves. Let us, therefore, in the genuine spirit of Christianity pray God to forgive them, and to turn their hearts.[95]

Otey appointed each Friday to be observed as a day of fasting, humiliation and prayer to Almighty God in order to seek forgiveness of sins, protection for the new Confederate nation and protection for the soldiers in the fields against all those who wished to oppress the Confederacy. He copied selections of the Psalms to be circulated among the soldiers in order to boost morale and provide assurance. He even labeled certain selections for reading just prior to a battle and selections to offer praise for the expected victories ahead. Otey placed his hope and confidence in God alone to deliver success and bring victory to what he viewed as a righteous cause.

Bishop Stephen Elliott served as a more tenacious bishop, articulating his views of Southern righteousness and Northern paganism and sounding the trumpet for war in the years preceding 1861 and only intensifying his rhetoric as the years progressed. Elliott served as the bishop of the Diocese of Georgia and as senior bishop of the Confederacy following the death of Bishop Otey of Tennessee. He, along with Bishop and General Leonidas Polk and Bishop Charles Quintard, was instrumental in establishing The University of the South at Sewanee, Tennessee. Elliott traveled throughout Tennessee during the Civil War preaching to the soldiers of the Army of Tennessee, and he published an extensive number of sermons addressing what he perceived to be the righteous nature of the conflict. He was one

The Right Reverend Stephen Elliott. *Courtesy of the University Archives and Special Collections, The University of the South.*

of the most ardent fire-eaters and was unrelenting in his passion and drive to carry forth his envisioned divine Confederate message.

During a visit in June 1863 to Shelbyville, Elliott baptized and confirmed Confederate general Braxton Bragg in the Episcopal Church. Quintard, chaplain to General Polk, visited General Bragg at his headquarters, claiming it "a matter of life and death." After assuring that the two men would be alone and undisturbed, Quintard ministered to Bragg about the importance of salvation and having Christ, especially for one in such a responsible position. After noticing that Bragg's eyes had flooded with tears, Quintard asked him if he would be confirmed. The general's reply was, "I have been waiting for twenty years to have someone say this to me, and I thank you from my heart. Certainly, I shall be confirmed if you will give me the necessary instruction."[96] Quintard was present while Bishop Elliott held the confirmation. During this same journey, at Wartrace, in May 1863, Elliott spoke to about five thousand soldiers.

Bishop Elliott believed that as an ordinary rule, the church should have little to do with political events. The circumstances in 1861, however, were far from ordinary. Thus, in an address to the thirty-ninth annual convention of the Protestant Episcopal Church in 1861, Elliott stated that although the Episcopal Church had never allowed the bitter strife of the evangelical denominations to enter into its consecrated walls, some type of separation from the North could not be avoided. Elliott believed that "amid the present confusion and distraction of the country, the Episcopal church could lift up clean hands and a pure heart and appeal to the God of Heaven that she has had no part nor lot, as a church, in producing the strife which was rapidly marching to dip its feet in blood."[97] At the same time, he acknowledged that the church could no longer remain independent of the political state of affairs. It was involved in politics even though the church, he claimed, did not have a hand in producing the issues. He further promoted the popular Confederate belief that the Confederacy was inherently Christian in its actions. He stated, "When the Commonwealth, as in our times, is, if not professedly, at least practically, Christian, it is almost impossible to draw any line which can separate the relations of the Church from the relations of the Commonwealth."[98]

In an 1862 sermon in Savannah, Georgia, and as

An early photograph of Confederate General Braxton Bragg. *Courtesy of the Library of Congress.*

part of a nationally proclaimed day of fasting and humiliation, Elliott noted, "The race is not to the swift, nor the battle to the strong, but our trust is in the name of the Lord our God."[99] He praised God for safely bringing the Confederacy to the close of its first year of political existence and asked for a continuance of the blessing that he believed God had granted the young Confederacy. Elliott pointed out that the Confederacy's whole future would depend upon these early years of political existence. Elliott further announced that the revolution could only be accomplished through a "baptism of blood." This "baptism" was necessary to redeem the moral degradation that Elliott believed to have taken over the North. He stated, "I affirm that this revolution was as much a moral as a political necessity. There is no instance upon record of such a rapid moral deterioration of a nation as has taken place in ours in the last forty years."[100] While abolitionists in the North were pointing to the immorality of slave ownership, Confederates envisioned only their superior morality, which they compared to the "irreligious" people of the North who Elliott argued were "lovers of pleasure rather than lovers of God." In discussing the Confederacy, Elliott stated, "We are at least a nation of Theists—men who recognize the presence of God in the affairs of the world. That is a point gained; a step out of darkness into light; and for that He may bless us and give us more light."[101] Elliott, nonetheless, revealed concern, and he concurred with the message of Tennessee army chaplain R.F. Bunting by disclosing an account of the mindset lodged in the Confederate soul following the 1861 victories. Elliott claimed:

> We have been manifesting, as a consequence of our repeated victories, a spirit of presumption, which is very much akin to the sin of saying—"My power and the might of mine hand hath gotten me this victory." Immediately after our great and signal victory at Manassas, God was in all our thoughts; we praised Him, we magnified Him, we glorified Him, we gave thanks to His most glorious majesty for His wonderful interposition in our behalf; but as time has rolled on, the arm of flesh has been gradually taking the place, in our language at least, if not in our thoughts, of the power of God. We have been hearing, of late, a great deal more about the skill of our Generals, about the valor of our troops, about the cowardice of our foes, than about God as our shield and defense. We have talked as if all that was necessary to victory, was that our troops should be let loose upon our enemies, and as if He, who ruleth in all the armies of the sky, had nothing to do with success or defeat. No spirit can be more fatal to us than this, for while it is especially hateful to God, it is the very worst policy in the world to despise one's enemies. We should have proper confidence in ourselves; we should go into battle praying and trusting that we may be victorious, but the moment that we consider victory as necessarily chained to our chariot wheels, we are in imminent danger both from God and man—from God because He will not have His glory given to another, and from man, "because pride goeth before destruction, and an haughty spirit before a fall." If we cherish this vain glorious temper, God will assuredly lay His hand upon those very things of which we make our boast—will take away our brave and skilful commanders by the edge of the sword. He is leading us by His own way to our independence and rest.[102]

This argument was resurrected by several ministers following the death of General "Stonewall" Jackson in May 1863, in response to the idolization of this talented commander. Elliott maintained, "What we need in this sacred conflict, is deep earnestness, religious enthusiasm, a solemn sense of responsibility, a devotedness to the right and the true. The value of

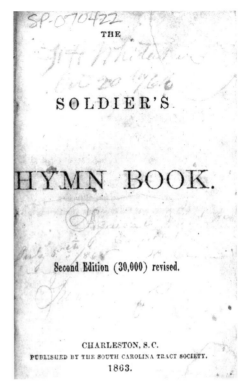

THE

SOLDIER'S

HYMN BOOK.

Second Edition (30,000) revised.

CHARLESTON, S.C.
PUBLISHED BY THE SOUTH CAROLINA TRACT SOCIETY.
1863.

Published in 1863, this songbook entitled *The Soldier's Hymn Book* was a source of inspiration and consolation to soldiers on the battlefield. *Courtesy of the Center for Popular Music, Middle Tennessee State University.*

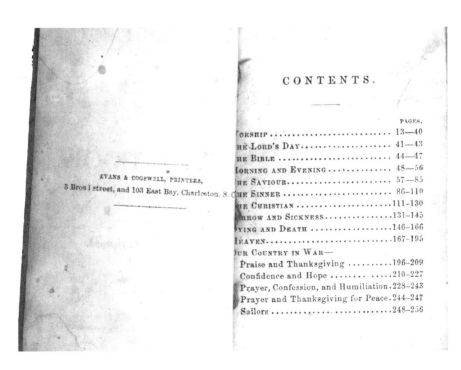

EVANS & COGSWELL, PRINTERS,
3 Broad street, and 103 East Bay, Charleston, S. C.

CONTENTS.

troops, of arms, of fortification, depends upon the courage of those who use them; upon the strength of heart which is behind them—and that comes from God."[103]

Elliott denunciated the North with fiery rhetoric, in which he consistently professed the North evil and the Confederate cause holy. The bishop foresaw the Northern "hordes of lawless men" and the ravages of a war, which sought the desolation of Southern homes, altars and families as the perilous times foretold in the Bible for the latter days. Christian soldiers of the Confederacy, who became casualties, would be remembered as martyrs in a holy cause. Elliott's prayer introduced powerful stereotypes to justify Confederate martyrdom. He declared:

> *If this were a mere struggle for political power, a question of sovereignty and of dominion, then should I be loath to mingle the Church of Christ with it in any form or manner, but such is not the nature of this conflict. It is no such war as nations wage against each other for a balance of power, or for the adjustment of a boundary. We are resisting a crusade—a crusade of license against law—of infidelity against the altars of the living God—of fanaticism against a great spiritual trust committed to our care. We are warring with hordes of unprincipled foreigners, ignorant and brutal men, who, having cast off at home all the restraints of order and of belief, have signalized their march over our devoted country by burning the Churches of Christ by defiling the altars upon which the sacrifice of the death of our Savior is commemorated, by violating our women, by raising the banner of servile insurrection, by fanning into fury the demoniac passions of the ignorant and the vile.[104]*

The bishop believed Christ had prepared His servant, the Confederacy, to resist this perceived invasion of Northern irreligion, ungodliness, corruption and cruelty.

Elliott used religious language to describe every aspect of war. He returned thanks to God for the "brilliant victories" given the "gallant soldiers of the South over the invaders of their soil." He prayed for deliverance from the "polluting tread of the enemy," and he labeled the Southern dead as martyrs in a sacred struggle. He announced that all were willing to suffer as needed for the sake of the cause because God had granted Confederates a willing mind. Elliott boasted of the Southern oneness while scoffing at the Northern zeal for war, one that, he predicted, would change from a war for union to a war for emancipation. Despite the obstacles, Elliott, with his envisioned unity of purpose, foresaw only victory. He claimed:

> *While many other motives are urging us to the battlefield, and we rush forward to defend our liberties, our homes, our altars, God is super-adding this other motive—the secret of His own will—is making it to produce within us, unconsciously perhaps to ourselves, a power which is irresistible. Our conscience in this war is thus made right towards God and towards man; our heart is filled with his fear and His love; our arm is nerved with almost super-human strength, and we have reason to thank Him, not only for what he has done for us, but for what he has restrained us from doing for ourselves and others from doing for us. This noble cause had made Him our guide and our overruling governor, and we are moving forward, as I firmly believe, as truly under his direction, as did the people of Israel when he led them with a pillar of cloud by day and of fire by night.*[105]

Elliott maintained that the institution of slavery was one of the sacred charges given to the South but threatened by the North. Christ-ordained slavery was a primary doctrine in the Confederate Episcopal Church, as well as in the Southern evangelical denominations. Historian Drew Gilpin-Faust discovered Confederates believed that the central component of the mission God had designed for the South was for Southerners to function as guardians and champions for a "heathen race."[106] Southern Christians, furthermore, believed the Bible sanctioned both slavery and the culture of the South, but it foretold judgment on societies that violated the sacred trust of Christian slavery.[107] The need to convert African American slaves was the primary justification for the institution of slavery. From the pulpit, sermons resounded regarding the slave owner's Christian duty to his slaves. Elliott forcefully proclaimed this sacred trust of slavery he believed the Almighty had bestowed on the Southern nation for the advancement of the slave. He asserted:

> *We believe that we are educating these people as they are educated no where else; that we are elevating them in every generation; that we are working out God's purposes, whose consummation we are quite willing to leave in his hands. We do not expect infidels—men who are clamoring for a new God, and a new Christ, and a new Bible—to believe this, but we did hope that Christian men, our brethren in the faith of Christ, and in the hopes of eternity, would credit our integrity and our faithfulness.*[108]

Elliott contended that the founding fathers had forced slaves on the South, and the South had rescued them from evil hands and "made men and

Christians" out of them. Elliott espoused that paganism would accompany freedom for the slaves, meaning that their race could perish in a civilized world. Elliott warned the North that they had profaned religion by seducing and then consigning slaves to misery. He left justice and vengeance to God, but he further proclaimed his church's intention to sacrifice everything in order to carry out its sacred charge. The Presbyterian minister James Henley Thornwell, one of the South's most respected theological leaders, concurred:

> *We feel that the souls of our slaves are a solemn trust, and we shall strive to present them faultless and complete before the presence of God. Indeed, as we contemplate their condition in the Southern States, and contrast it with that of their fathers before them, and that of their brethren in the present day in their native land, we cannot but accept it as a gracious Providence that they have been brought in such numbers to our shores, and redeemed from the bondage of barbarism and sin.*[109]

Ministers justified their cries for a religious war on biblical scripture, which the South used with an expertise that far outweighed that of the abolitionists.[110] The doctrine of divinely sanctioned slavery hinged on the Confederate interpretation of the "slavery scriptures." The Southern clergy believed the Old Testament provided a strong case for slavery, and they exploited numerous scriptures from books of both testaments. Israelites—including Abraham and the other great patriarchs—were slave owners. In the New Testament, neither Jesus nor the apostles ever preached against slavery even though the institution surrounded them. The Apostle Paul admonished Christians on the proper way to treat their slaves. The Noahic curse—they believed—provided the racial justification for black slaves in particular, but the basic argument for divine slavery was not supposed to be racial.[111] Old and New Testament societies were most often slave societies, and that fact was enough for most clergy. The scripture "Think not that I come to send peace on the Earth, but a sword" also proved to be popular for justification of battle, and the Book of Psalms received near constant usage for morale. "O Lord arise, help us and deliver us, for thy name's sake" was a common battle cry.[112]

Along with scriptural justification, once again, Confederates drew a comparison between themselves and the North, and once again, Southerners placed themselves on the moral high road, believing that Southern bondage was far superior to Northern wage slavery. Following defeat, Confederates reluctantly recognized that their angry God had used "infidels" to punish His chosen for their disobedience. To the planter aristocracy, the demise of slavery did not invalidate their certainty that God had ordained it in a previous time and place.[113] Elite Southerners were committed to the way of life that slavery made possible and therefore embraced the scriptures for religious justification.

Elliott prayed that God would receive glory for Confederate victories through an advancement of the gospel, honor of the country and good to all mankind. He claimed that the Lord was smiting the "insulting and vain-glorious nation" of the United States. As the war continued, however, Elliott felt pressed to explain defeats on the battlefields, especially throughout Tennessee. He explained:

> *But God has thought it best for us that this cruel war should endure yet longer and should be waged with an increased ferocity. Our sins are to be more heavily punished, at the same time that our faith is to be more thoroughly sifted, and our submission to his will made more complete and perfect. The causes which led to this war—many of the circumstances which have accompanied it and the marvelous manifestations of himself which God has made throughout it—the mighty interests of a moral and religious nature which are bound up in its results—all forbid us from looking upon it as a mere conflict for power. We must take the Divine will into all our reasonings about it, and our humiliation to-day must occupy itself in helping us to school ourselves into an acquiescence with his divine arrangements. We may feel sure, seeing how visibly He has fought for us—how strikingly He has supported us through our hours of mortal peril—how He has strengthened us in our weakness, and comforted us in our desolation—that whatever He may order for us in the conduct of this struggle, shall be for our ultimate blessing, and that we ourselves shall one day see it and confess it.[114]*

Elliott worried that political leaders would hasten to procure a peace settlement, possibly through foreign mediation. He sternly warned against rushing to a peace prior to God accomplishing His divine purpose. He maintained that the sins of the South could delay deliverance in their "revolution" for years to come, but if so, this was a vital delay. Just as the Israelites had wandered in the desert for forty years in order to receive discipline, the South, too, needed discipline. He argued that without this discipline and purification, a country could not endure. Elliott shamed leaders seeking peace by reminding them of the economic, political and social inequities existing between the two sections of the country before the war, and he further reminded them of the bravery of the tens of thousands of soldiers who, for the sake of duty and patriotism, marched fearlessly to battle. He stated that the Confederacy hoped, prayed and struggled for victory, pressing on, knowing everything was in the hands of God. Quoting DeRanville, he proclaimed, "If the genius of evil is to prove triumphant, if legitimate government is again to fall, let it at least fall with honor; shame alone has no future."[115]

Elliott further defended the all-too-common defeats of the Confederate army by declaring, "The odds against us were too great, unless we believed that God was on our side, and that His influences would equalize the conflict. Almost every six months since this struggle commenced, have we bowed ourselves, as a people, before the Lord of Hosts, and prayed for his mercy and protection from the fury of our mighty foes."[116] As defeats visited the armies, the tone even of a fire-eater such as Elliott grew slightly less rabid. Reality replaced the language of miracles. In 1864, Elliott explained, "God works by means; we must not expect in these days, to receive help from Him through miracle. He will help us in time of trouble, but through ordinary means. He will help us by giving us strength in the day of adversity; by opening our hearts to sustain our government; by quelling dissensions among ourselves; by infusing courage into all those who are weak-minded and timid; by confounding the devices of our enemies."[117]

No matter how gloomy prospects for victory might have appeared, Elliott never lost faith in the end result of the war. By the summer of 1863, Elliott admitted that God "might try severely our fortitude—He might chasten heavily our sins—He might keep us long in the furnace of affliction, but in the end, He would deliver us and justify our trust in Him."[118] Midway through 1864, he stated, "I have full confidence in the successful termination of this conflict. What we may suffer in the struggle is one thing; the end of the struggle is quite another thing. This is God's war; He has conducted it upon very remarkable principles; and He will terminate it in His own way."[119]

The ministers of the Evangelical churches operating within the Confederacy equaled the passion and determination of Episcopal ministers Bishops Polk, Otey and Elliott. The first Baptist church to be organized in a Virginia city and the first church of any denomination to be organized in Richmond, the historic First Baptist Church of Richmond conducted its first meeting in 1780. From 1854 through 1874, Reverend John Lansing Burrows served as the pastor of the First Baptist Church. Following the battle in Tennessee at Shiloh, Burrows delivered a sermon entitled "Shiloh," which he published and distributed in tract form. Regardless of the actual outcome of the battle, to the minister, Shiloh was a distinct victory. He claimed, "Shiloh, is henceforth to be one of precious names in the history of the Confederate States. With it will be associated as with those other names, derived from the Holy scriptures, Bethel and Manassas, the idea of victory—God given victory."[120]

Burrows, like many other ministers, including Elliott, blamed recent defeats on the failure of the Confederate soldiers to fully acknowledge the Lord as their source for victory. He proposed that the initial victory at Manassas had a special significance based on its location, which was chosen by Providence. Manassas in the Bible meant "causing to forget." Joseph, the son of Jacob, had named his child Manassas after achieving a position of authority in Egypt after his brothers sold him to the Egyptians as a slave years earlier. Joseph believed God had given him reason to forget his sufferings. Likewise, Burrows argued the Confederacy had suffered at the hands of the United States government and God was preparing them

This illustration depicts Confederate chaplain and prominent Southern Baptist leader Dr. John Lansing Burrows preaching in his shirtsleeves near Harrisonburg, Virginia, in the summer of 1863. Dr. Burrows's coat was stolen on his way to church. He is reported to have said, "Well, if you and your people can stand my filing your pulpit in this garb, I reckon I can." *Courtesy of the Southern Baptist Historical Library and Archives, Nashville, Tennessee.*

for victory that would cause them to forget their past unfair treatment. The Confederate soldiers, however, had allowed themselves to become puffed up in their own strength following this mighty victory, and thus, God had to chastise them, his children. He stated, "Manassas did cause us to forget, too guiltily, that our strength and dependence were in God. In our exultation we forgot our trust, in our pride we forgot the humility which God loveth."[121] Once again, a clergyman argued against idolizing the Confederate heroes such as "Stonewall" Jackson, comparing this worship to the pagan idols of the Old Testament.

Shiloh, according to Burrows, represented more than the Lord's chastisement of the Confederate nation. Burrows asserted that Shiloh brought to the Confederates what they had desired. He proclaimed:

> *This victory we have been praying for earnestly, devoutly, tearfully, in the closet, at the family altar, in the church, and in our daily prayer meetings. He who heareth the cry of His children, hath listened in pity to our importunities and hath given us Shiloh—what we have desired and prayed for. Brethren, is there not a connection between the prayers of God's people and the victory we have gained. All over this land, Christians have prayed in penitent earnestness, have gotten hold of the arm of Jehovah, and brought it down upon our enemy's heads. What we longed for has been granted. We prayed for it and God has given us Shiloh—the desired.*[122]

The Tennessee Monument on Shiloh Battlefield was dedicated on June 3, 2004, to commemorate the services of nearly 14,200 men from Tennessee, along with several dozen Tennesseans in Union regiments from Illinois, Ohio and Kentucky, who fought in the Battle of Shiloh on April 6 and 7, 1862. More than 3,220 Tennesseans were killed, wounded or missing in the battle. *Author's collection.*

To the soldiers who fought in and near what they termed "The Bloody Pond" and "The Hornet's Nest," despite Burrows's claims to the contrary, this battle probably did not represent what they desired most.

Burrows next translated Shiloh as "the tranquilizer" or "the pacification." In other words, he believed God was delivering peace to the Confederate nation. Shiloh, predicted Burrows, was the beginning in a series of victories that would deliver peace to the beleaguered country. He claimed that all nations must endure strife and could find peace only after hardships and battle. Burrows proclaimed:

> *We are fighting for peace. We want peace for ourselves and we are anxious to live in peace with our neighbors and the world. Oh! What joy it would bring to our suffering and distracted land, if this etymological signification of the name Shiloh, could be answered, and that bloody battle field prove the Pacificator from which should issue the negotiations which sooner or later must come, that shall result in the recognition of our indisputable right to self government, in the cessation of hostilities and the restoration of*

"The Drummer Boy of Shiloh," a ballad written and composed by Will Shakespeare Hays, tells the story of a drummer boy who met his death in that battle. The ballad reads in part, "Look down upon the battle field, Oh, Thou our Heavenly Friend! Have mercy on our sinful souls! The soldiers cried, 'Amen!'" *Courtesy of the Center for Popular Music, Middle Tennessee State University.*

peace. We hail with joy the omens, which this name suggest and will pray that they may be fulfilled.[123]

Burrows sadly recalled the losses of Forts Henry and Donelson in February 1862, noting that the cause was as equally just and righteous there as it was at Manassas but reminding his listeners that God disciplines his children through affliction, trials and sufferings. Reverses, he believed, brought humility and a greater dependence on an Almighty God, prerequisites to victory. He argued that God would bring Southern independence, but He would never leave the Confederacy independent from God Himself. He explained what had been accomplished up to this point through Confederate dependence on God:

> *Our remorseless enemies, confident and boastful of greater numbers and superior resources, have been reluctantly compelled to admit over again the divine apothegm, "The battle is not always to the strong." God has appeared for us, and our marshaled forces, condemned and ridiculed, as too few and weak for effective resistance to such numbers and might—as dissolute and ragged and ignorant and miserably armed—have held the braggart foe at bay for more than a year. Through God's favor we have driven his efficiently equipped armies from many a battlefield and at this hour hold them in check at all their selected points of assault. We cannot attribute these mercies, to greater numbers, to ampler resources, to more effective implements of war, to superior drill and discipline, for in all we have been inferior. To what then shall we attribute it? The text is the answer—"The Lord hath appeared" for us.*[124]

Finally, Burrows argued that in the same manner that Shiloh meant a reappearing of the Lord in Old Testament times, the greatest element of the "victory" at Shiloh was that the "God of Battles" had revisited the Confederate army. Burrows acknowledged that Shiloh had not been a decisive victory, and he greatly lamented the loss of so many lives, Union and Confederate, paying special tribute to the highest-ranking casualty, General Albert Sidney Johnston. The reverend, nonetheless, rejoiced that the battle had proved the Lord was the Confederate army's "shield and defense." He proclaimed, "An army comparatively poorly clad and poorly armed, has met and mastered an army of at least equal numbers, said to have been one of the best equipped and prepared for battle that the world has ever seen. What other conclusion can we reach than this—the God of battles favored our cause?"[125]

The Methodist churches also fostered a belief in the sacred nature of the Confederate cause and the supreme necessity of receiving divine

This log Methodist church, known as Shiloh Church, gave the Battle of Shiloh its name. Biblically known as "place of peace," Shiloh Church was the site of some of the fiercest fighting yet seen in the Civil War. *Courtesy of the Library of Congress.*

intervention in order for a nation to prosper. According to Methodist minister George Foster Pierce, in a sermon delivered before the Bible Convention of the Confederate States in Augusta, Georgia, in 1862, the crime and curse of America stemmed from the blessings of God, which too many took for granted. He claimed, "We have prospered, grown rich, luxurious, proud, and have said in our hearts, my power and the might of my hand hath gotten me this wealth."[126] To conserve the nation, he argued for complete submission to God, in the constitution, in the system of education and in the lifestyles of the inhabitants, especially in the soldiers in the camps. His message to the soldiers simply stated, "Let us remember that our country is to be preserved and perpetuated, not by science, wealth, patriotism, population, armies, or navies, but by every word that proceedeth out of the mouth of the Lord."[127]

According to historian David B. Chesebrough, ministers reflected the current thought and practice of a society. The popularity of certain preachers compared to the lesser-accomplished or well-known ministers disclosed the messages that were popular with the public at the time. The parishioners shaped the clergy just as the clergy shaped the parishioners. Chesebrough claimed, "It would be difficult for a clergyman to survive in his vocation if he did not share to a large degree the values and sentiments of his congregation." Sermons, therefore, reflected current thinking, problems and issues that occupied the attention and emotions of a large number of people.[128] Chesebrough further explained:

> *In warfare, the preachers proclaimed, it was not the number of soldiers, nor the competency of generals that determined the tide of battle; it was God who brought victory and it was God who administered defeat. Therefore, no matter how bleak a present situation might be, or how disastrous the latest defeat suffered on the battlefield, there was always hope. God could change everything, suddenly and dramatically, if He so desired. So the bloodshed and killing continued in the Civil War long after defeat seemed obvious; for God was the God of history, the God who still worked miracles upon the world's stage, the God who brought forth the impossible, the God who could easily turn heartbreaking defeat into glorious victory.[129]*

According to James Silver, following the defeats at Vicksburg and Gettysburg, the clergy preached and distributed a deluge of sermons addressing the sins of the Confederate people. These sins alone, ministers argued, would bring defeat to the Confederate cause. Reverend Burrows also explained that although the sins of the South were no greater than the sins of other nations, more was required of Southerners because of their special status as God's chosen people.

To Bishops Otey and Elliott of the Confederate Episcopal Church, Reverend Burrows of the First Baptist Church and Reverend Pierce of the Methodist Church, the Civil War was God's war. All envisioned the war as both a revolution against tyranny and a defensive war wielded to protect Southern homes, property and life. Elliott spoke for the majority of ministers by expressing the inherent righteousness of the South. Through the war, God would create a holy peculiar nation like He had previously done with the Israelites. Victory from God would present itself in the form of an independent Confederate States of America. To Otey and Burrows, however, the South was filled with sinners who had turned their backs on God and His laws. Through the war, God would create holy individuals from the trials and temptations of war. Victory would present itself in a crown of righteousness granted for eternity. The issue of "divine slavery" was most important to the minority aristocracy in their reasoning for the war. Regardless of the particular message, the Southern clergy took advantage of the centrality of religion to Southern life, and from the church house to the statehouse, the clergy led the way into secession and war.

CHAPTER 4

CHAPLAINS IN THE ARMY OF TENNESSEE, CSA

Disciples Carrying the Gospel

No righteous cause, when supported in the fear of God can possibly be lost, unless abandoned.
—*Reverend R.F. Bunting, March 20, 1862*

Throughout our nation's history, from the foundation of the republic to the present day, a debate has raged over religion's place in the public sphere. In 1861, the United States was the most Christian nation in the world, and throughout the Civil War, the number of converts to Christianity continued to rise. Unlike any other time before or since, the United States was "one nation, under God."[130] Religious language and symbolism were commonplace throughout the war era in public politics, published sermons and journalism. Abraham Lincoln noted the irony of the country's religious fervor in his second inaugural address as president of the United States. He observed, "Both read the same Bible, and pray to the same God; and each invokes His aid against the other. The prayers of both could not be answered—that of neither has been answered fully."[131]

The Civil War forged a religious national identity. The strongest evidence of this existed in the extensive work of the army chaplains and in the accompanying vast and sweeping religious revivals. These revivals rapidly spread through both the Northern and Southern armies during the war, with the Southern armies experiencing the greatest revival outpouring. During the Civil War period, officials commissioned over six hundred chaplains in the Confederate army.[132] According to historian Herman Norton in *Religion in Tennessee 1777–1945*, the vast majority of Tennessee chaplains

This illustration depicts United States President Abraham Lincoln reading the Bible to his son. *Courtesy of the Library of Congress.*

served with Confederate units. Responding to the challenge to combat the evil and vice customarily associated with military life, chaplains came from every Christian denomination in Tennessee to enlist in the Army of Tennessee, CSA.[133] The army chaplains who ministered to battle-hardened soldiers were worlds removed from the lives of most of the elite Confederate clergy. They "lived, ate, marched, and suffered beside the soldiers to whom they preached."[134]

It was considered a disgrace for anyone to enter the ministry after the war began due to the perception that these ministers were attempting to avoid combat. Historian Walter Fleming noted, "By law, ministers were exempt from military service, but nearly all of the able-bodied ministers went to the war as chaplains, or as officers, leading the men of their congregations."[135] Ministers were expected to fight like all other Southern men.

Among the many Tennessee ministers who served as chaplains to the Army of Tennessee, CSA, was Bishop Charles Todd Quintard of the Episcopal Church. Quintard served as chaplain general to the Confederate army, and because he was a bishop of the Diocese of Tennessee, he had the opportunity to minister to many leaders and soldiers throughout the Army of Tennessee. Quintard, along with Bishops Leonidas Polk and Stephen Elliott, was one of the founders of The University of the South prior to the war. During the war, he joined with the common soldiers in the field to minister as an army chaplain, and he authored the book *The Confederate Soldier's Pocket Manual of Devotions.*

Ironically, Quintard was born in Stanford, Connecticut, and was educated in Northern schools. He attended Trinity School, New York City, and Columbia College. He received from Columbia his master's degree and graduated in 1847 with the degree of doctor of medicine from the University of the City of New York. Following a year at Bellevue Hospital, Quintard moved to Georgia and practiced medicine in Athens. In 1857, he accepted the chair of physiology and anatomy at the medical college in Memphis, Tennessee.[136] While in Memphis, Quintard met Bishop Otey, and within three years, Quintard was studying for the ministry. Following his ordination, the doctor served as rector of the Church of the Advent in Nashville, Tennessee, and further served at other nearby parishes.

In 1859, the Rock City Guard, a militia company, was organized in Nashville. The group asked Quintard to

The Right Reverend Charles Todd Quintard of the Episcopal Church served as chaplain general to the Confederate army and was a bishop of the Diocese of Tennessee. *Courtesy of the Library of Congress.*

serve as its chaplain, a foreshadowing of his service yet to come. When war commenced in 1861, the Rock City Guard took Quintard with them to fight the war. Initially, Quintard served in Virginia and became a close friend of General Robert E. Lee. Among his congregants in the fields were both Generals Lee and "Stonewall" Jackson.[137] In 1862, Quintard returned to Tennessee and resumed his position as chaplain with the First Tennessee Volunteer Regiment, Army of Tennessee, CSA. Besides his ministry, he further offered his service as a surgeon to wounded soldiers.

Quintard commanded the respect of and was favored with intimate relationships among Southerners from all levels of the Confederate government and military. On June 14, 1862, Quintard received a letter from President Jefferson Davis appointing him chaplain general in the Provisional

Army in the service of the Confederate States.[138] Quintard met with and actually slept under the same blanket with General Polk on the Perryville battlefield, and during a day of truce in the church at Harrodsburg, Kentucky, Quintard held prayers with both Polk and General Edmund Kirby-Smith. Quintard also presented General Braxton Bragg to Bishop Elliott for confirmation. General Bragg wrote Quintard in June 1864 thanking him for *The Confederate Soldier's Pocket Manual of Devotions* that he had received. Quintard received continual correspondence from members of the clergy, the military and political leaders thanking him for the work that he was accomplishing in the Confederate army.

The Right Reverend Charles Todd Quintard. *Courtesy of the University Archives and Special Collections, The University of the South.*

A transplanted Northerner, Quintard rallied to the Confederate cause, and he encouraged the troops to give their all for their righteous crusade. His most famous sermon, which was published and widely distributed throughout the Confederate army, was "Samson Sermon." In camp near Chattanooga on August 10, 1862, Quintard preached this sermon before the First Tennessee Regiment. He declared:

> *In the name of God I summon you to conflict and victory. In all your manliness stand forth and enlist under Christ's banner. As men you will be all the truer; as soldiers all the better and the braver. I know not what may be before you. In the hour of your country's need you may mark out a lofty and heroic career. Amid the rush of battle, calm and controlled, you may win for yourselves honor among your fellows. With an heroic heart you may bind your life to duty, and when destruction rushes dreadful to the field and bathes itself in blood, you may bear your country's banner with a firm hand and an unflinching heart. And if your soul is stayed on God, come life or come death, your victory shall be sure.*[139]

Quintard, like so many Southern ministers, drew a connection between protecting home and protecting the altar of Christ. As with the Southern gentleman ideal of the antebellum period, God and honor were undeniably and eternally joined together. In this view, one could not live as a Christian and not protect one's family and one's home. In a memorial for Captain Thomas Edward King, who died at the Battle of Chickamauga in 1863, Quintard wrote:

> *His life was rendered illustrious by an exhibition of all those virtues which adorn the patriot and the Christian. He was brave without temerity, generous without prodigality, noble without pride, and virtuous without severity. Wounded at the battle of Manassas, on the 21st of July 1861, he was unable to resume the command of his company, but when his native state was threatened he felt that he must join the struggle to drive the invader from his altar and his home. He accepted a position on the staff of the gallant General Preston Smith and fell with him, at the close of the day, cheerfully offering up his life for his country's cause.*[140]

The carefully selected words of the clergy, such as "offering up his life," further emphasized the Christian sacrificial ideal of giving one's life for the cause.

Quintard's *The Confederate Soldier's Pocket Manual of Devotions* was circulated throughout the Confederate army. The manual consisted of ninety-six pages of specifically designed prayers. The manual included specific prayers for particular events in the soldier's life. Quintard prepared prayers for camp settings, prayers to be offered just prior to battle, prayers of praise for victory and prayers for aid in suffering and defeat, among several other situations of a soldier's experience. For example, Quintard penned a prayer designed to offer hope for an impending victory. He wrote:

PRAYER, AND HOPE OF VICTORY

Now may the God of grace and power
Attend His people's humble cry;
Defend them in the needful hour,
And send deliverance from on high.

In His salvation is our hope;
And in the name of Israel's God
Our troops shall lift their banners up,
Our Navies spread their flags abroad.

Some trust in horses trained for war,
And some of chariots make their boast;
Our surest expectations are
From Thee, the Lord of Heavenly Hosts.

Then save us, Lord, from slavish fear,
And let our trust be firm and strong,
Till Thy salvation shall appear,
And hymns of peace conclude our song.[141]

Quintard's prayers frequently requested protection for the "humble" South against the assaults of its enemies. He further sought divine aid from a God who, Quintard boasted, did not always give the battle to the strong. Quintard petitioned the Lord to take the cause into His own hands and judge between the two nations, resting assured that the judgment of the Lord would come down on the side of the Confederacy. Quintard imploringly beseeched the Almighty to offer His blessings on "Thy servant, the President of the Confederate States, and all others in authority."[142]

Manual of Devotion by Thomas Frank Gailor. In an 1899 memorial address, the Right Reverend Gailor described Quintard's years of service to Sewanee as "no finer chapter in the history of the American Church." *Courtesy of the University Archives and Special Collections, The University of the South.*

Throughout his manual, he described the troops as soldiers of the cross who sought courage for the glorious war that would surely bring victory both in the present life and in the hereafter. In order to relate to the condition of the common soldier, he made comparisons between the Lord's sufferings and the current sufferings being endured by the bedraggled army. In a prayer concerning rest, Quintard wrote, "My feet are worn and weary with the march over rough roads and up the steep hill-side." He followed this stanza with, "Patience, poor soul; thy Saviour's feet were worn; The Saviour's heart and hands were weary too; His garments stained, and travel-worn, and old; his sacred eyes blinded with tears for you."[143] Throughout his sermons, writings and prayers, Quintard emphasized the dire need for courage and patience, firmly believing that God, in the end, following a spiritual renewing of the troops, would prove himself faithful by establishing victory and independence for the Confederate people.

An example of a lesser-known yet equally steadfast believer in God and the Confederate cause was Chaplain Henry Daniel Polk Hogan. Hogan was born on April 29, 1840, in Nashville, Tennessee. Throughout his childhood, he lived with his family in a five-room log cabin on their three-hundred-acre farm, which was located about seven miles south of Nashville. Hogan had eight siblings, and although he received several years of education in Maury County, Tennessee, he and his siblings worked on their family farm. The family owned one slave, but the family would also hire three or four more slaves at times to help them with their work. Hogan matured in an environment where hard labor was respected, and all were expected to work regardless of color, class or condition of servitude.

Hogan enlisted in the Confederate army on April 29, 1861, on his twenty-first birthday, in Humphreys County, Tennessee. He enlisted in Company B, Twenty-fourth Tennessee Infantry, Strahl's Brigade, Cheatham's Division in the Army of Tennessee. He enrolled for a ten-month period initially, and he was mustered into Captain Samuel E. Shannon's Company of the Twenty-fourth Tennessee Infantry on August 24, 1861. Following his wounding at the Battle of Shiloh, where he had served as the color guard of the regimental flag, Hogan's minister friend, the Reverend J.W. Culom, resigned from the chaplainry and returned home, and Colonel John A. Wilson then appointed Hogan chaplain of his regiment.[144]

Hogan served at the Battle of Perryville and the Battle of Stones River. He suffered multiple wounds as a soldier, was taken prisoner and later exchanged and served as the chaplain to his regiment throughout the war. Hogan directed the construction of a place to hold religious services while in winter quarters near Dalton, Georgia, and many volunteers worked to assemble the building. He preached the Gospel and stated that at every service the altar was filled with soldiers desiring to be converted. As a result of those services, Bishop Quintard baptized General Otho F. Strahl into the Episcopal Church. Following a battle southeast of Nashville on December 16, 1864, Reverend Hogan conducted Colonel James D. Tillman, then commanding

Reverend Henry Daniel Polk Hogan served as a soldier and chaplain in Company B, Twenty-fourth Regiment, of the Confederate Army of Tennessee. Seen here with the flag of his unit, this photograph was taken in 1929, when Hogan was eighty-nine years old, in Kansas City, Kansas. *Courtesy of Gerald and Helen (Williams) Miller. Helen Miller is the granddaughter of Reverend Hogan.*

Strahl's brigade, along with hundreds of his fellow soldiers, through territory familiar to him south of Nashville, thereby avoiding their capture by the Union army. Hogan claimed that a "special act of Providence" allowed him to save these men from capture and possible prison death.[145]

Late in the war, Hogan requested a transfer to Baxter's Battery in Macon, Georgia, in order to be near his younger brother following the death or capture of all of his original company. His captain, R.T. Tindall, approved his request. Tindall described Hogan as a "good and true soldier, having never missed but one engagement, always prompt to duty and obedient to orders."[146] Lieutenant General Richard Taylor, commander of the Army of Tennessee, subsequently denied his request. Hogan recalled, "One of the saddest days in my life was the 29th of April, 1865, just four years to the day from the date of my enlistment on my Twenty-First birthday, April 29th 1861, when I stacked my gun in surrender to W.T. Sherman at Greensboro, North Carolina, when I knew I was now helpless in the hands of a relentless foe."[147]

Confederate chaplain R.F. Bunting served the Army of Tennessee as an ardent fire-eater on the scale of Bishop Elliott. Bunting was chaplain to the Eighth Texas Cavalry, Terry's Regiment of Texas Rangers, which fought as part of the Army of Tennessee. He, too, served as both soldier and minister. The interest and attentiveness expressed by the soldiers to religious services comforted Bunting. He recounted, "When circumstances permit, we forget not the assembling of ourselves together in the groves for public worship. The attendance is large and the attention most encouraging."[148] Bunting stated that he was permitted to preach regularly on Sabbaths and that he endeavored to preach at the wagon trains in the morning and in the front of camp in the evening.

Bunting further addressed the Confederate chaplain's determination to acquire religious reading material for the Confederate troops. He frequently complained of the deficiency of army chaplains, as well as that of religious reading material. He contended that the soldiers appreciated the preaching in camp and that preaching along with religious tracts and Bibles achieved positive results in the soldiers'

Reverend Henry Daniel Polk Hogan enlisted in the Confederate Army of Tennessee on his twenty-first birthday on April 29, 1861. He stacked his gun in surrender on April 29, 1865, four years to the day of his enlistment, at Greensboro, North Carolina. This photograph of Hogan wearing his dress uniform was taken about 1924. *Courtesy of Gerald and Helen (Williams) Miller. Helen Miller is the granddaughter of Reverend Hogan.*

lives. His letters expressed these positive results and his early belief in victory for what he perceived as the Christian cause, as he remarked on January 4, 1862:

Our beginning has been in every respect most propitious, we recognize God's hand. God reigns; therefore, will we not fear. But we are not conquered with God on our side, though one and another noble leader may fall, yet there will be others to fill the breach, and although many of our generous-hearted and gallant boys may rest from the conflict, our invaders will yet be driven back; our homes and loved ones will be saved from ruin, and our independence will be achieved.[149]

Following the death of Lieutenant Colonel Thomas S. Lubbock, Bunting described a divine purpose in the taking of the lives of Southern leaders: "God will raise up other brave and noble spirits to lead us on to victory. It may indeed be that we loved our gallant leaders too well, that we trusted to their judgment and their bravery too much and now God has come and taken our idols from us, in order that we may not rely too much upon an arm of flesh, but trust more in Him."[150]

Following each of their deaths, Bunting also discussed the deaths of Generals "Stonewall" Jackson and Albert Sidney Johnston. The reverend joined with the Confederacy in mourning the deaths of the great "Christian heroes," and he recognized the irreparable damage their loss caused the

Reverend R.F. Bunting was sent as a missionary to Texas by the Presbyterian Church in 1851 and served pastorates at La Grange, Columbus and San Antonio, Texas, prior to the Civil War. In 1861, he was made chaplain of Terry's Texas Rangers, Eighth Texas Cavalry, which fought as part of the Army of Tennessee. He served as both soldier and minister during the Civil War. *Courtesy of the Tennessee State Library and Archives.*

Confederate South. Bunting, however, firmly reminded the soldiers that their trust was in God and not in men. He declared that soldiers were not to idolize men regardless of a leader's valor, success, popularity, deep piety or even his pure Christian patriotism. Troops were to respectfully remember the "soldiers of the cross" and emulate their virtues but not trust in the might of men for a Southern victory if the South was to achieve its independence. Bunting reminded his readers, "God can remove the chief of workmen, and still carry on the cause of liberty."[151]

Bunting drew encouragement from the scriptures, especially since in all cases in the Bible where the people of God humbled themselves and began to fast and pray, deliverance was experienced. Bunting described throughout his numerous letters the religious services taking place in the camps that he believed would bring into fruition the humility required for deliverance. He often expressed the irrelevancy of the enemy's numbers, weapons and supplies, noting that God controlled the winds and the waves, and He, thus, could cause His people to triumph. After several defeats and the abandonment of much Southern land, he described the Southern victory at Manassas as the "most disastrous battle" of all battles for the South. He maintained that this great victory worked to destroy humility within the hearts of Southerners, and humility was crucial to a Confederate cause that fully relied on divine favor. He believed the error that stemmed from that victory cost many lives and much property. Bunting described the turn of events in the following way:

> *We gloried in the victory and it was a magnificent triumph of arms. It was nobly achieved. But from a humble people, struggling for our rights, and looking to God for help, we at once became boastful and self-reliant. It was our own strong arms and brave hearts that had gotten us the victory; it was the splendid generalship of our own idolized commanders that had led forth our gallant troops, and made them triumphant. We overlooked the fact that there was a Providence in it. We forgot God in the exuberance of our joy. Now we hear nothing but retreats, evacuations, and advantages gained by our powerful enemy. There is cause for all of this. It comes not by chance or accident. God's providence is in it. We had forgotten Him. We were looking to other sources for aid. Our rulers were anticipating foreign alliances. But these failings and adversity coming upon us from every quarter, we turned back again to that <u>only source</u> from whence all our help cometh. Our people have been praying. They have been looking unto God in whom our Fathers trusted when the day of adversity was upon them. I feel encouraged for the future.*[152]

Bunting prayed for Southern leaders to gain wisdom, soldiers to be imbued with courage, victory to come to arms and peace to be attained for the Southern nation. His constant prayer was that the "God of Battles" would empower the Confederate troops so that they could meet the enemy and put him to flight. Bunting constantly reiterated that their trust was in the Lord and that with the Lord on their side, success was inevitable. If the Confederacy was not yet prepared for the solemn holy trust of independence, however, the reverend maintained, the war would continue until God had accomplished His work in the hearts of Southern men. As a result of his recognition of sin within the Confederacy, the reverend's outlook for the immediate future was grim, but he believed there would be a glorious end. He predicted a release for the South from the "heartless task-masters of Egypt" by declaring:

Our struggle may last for years. It may be fierce and bloody. There may be much to discourage, cities may be taken or destroyed, states may be overrun, armies may be defeated, the people may suffer every indignity and oppression. God may permit all those things, but our cause will triumph in the end. If we hold steadily and firmly in view the glorious cause which is the object of all endeavor, the goal of our highest ambition, the theme of our most earnest prayers and the consummation of our hopes, who can for a moment doubt that success will eventually crown our arms, and justify before the world the glorious and holy cause for which our Confederacy is nobly battling. No righteous cause, when supported in the fear of God <u>can possibly be lost</u>, unless <u>abandoned</u>. [153]

The hope for the Confederacy in 1862–63 was Lee's Army of Northern Virginia. God and religion also could be used to explain why the cause went so well in Virginia and so poorly in Tennessee. Bunting explained:

But the Lord of Hosts seems pre-eminently to bless the Army of Northern Virginia. Its guiding genius, General Lee, is a Christian. Its representative man, Stonewall Jackson, is a Christian. Many of its officers and men are Christians. May this not account for its unparalleled success? The world has never witnessed such a series of splendid victories before. God is recognizing that branch of our army in its sufferings and noble efforts for our young nation, and He is pouring down abundantly His spirit in the revival of His own work. Reports come to us that whole divisions are enjoying a season of refreshment from the presence of the Lord, and men are enquiring what they must do to be saved. We thank God for this token of His presence with us in our glorious struggle, for this evidence of his blessing upon us and our efforts. Would to God that we could say the same of this Western army. But we will not despair; the Holy Spirit may yet pass by this way and bless us. The seed has been sown in tears and in faith, and we yet wait and hope for the blessing. It is to be regretted, however, that many are careless, and that there is so much wickedness in camp, and so little that is good and virtuous. One great difficulty in the way—perhaps the greatest—arises from the fact that so very few of our officers are professors of religion. [154]

By other accounts, including his own, Bunting overstated the lack of faith at this time in the western theater. He, however, applauded the faith of the Southern governors leading the Confederacy.

Chaplains consistently looked to faith as the decisive element determining victory or defeat and continually spoke out against the camp sins that they believed contributed to their trials. Bunting wrote of the popularity of the Masonic order among the troops, which he proposed "inculcated universal benevolence and unbounded charity and encouraged every moral and social virtue, which introduced peace and good will among mankind and recommended itself to the philanthropist, the patriot, and the Christian."[155] Yet Bunting still found reason to complain. He lamented, "One sinner destroyeth much good and ruins many souls."[156] Bunting, however, continually looked to the "righteousness" of the cause and the biblical examples that directed him to a knowledge that the Confederacy could not fail. He explained:

> *We are merely standing on the defensive—we are asking to be left alone—our whole object is the defense of our homes, our families, our altars, our property. We can take encouragement in the matter. For when we read the Bible record, it will appear that in all those cases mentioned where God's people have sought and obtained His favor by fasting and prayer, it has been for deliverance from some terrible impending calamity. When were a people more threatened than ours? When has an enemy waged a more cruel, bitter, and fiendish war than this we now are engaged in? Hence the assurance if we call upon Him, He will hear us and bring us out safely through all these dangers that threaten our existence as a nation. With Him it matters not what their strength or prestige or courage may be. He can make the winds and waves the messengers of His will and bring us through every battle victorious.*[157]

Bunting reminded his readers of the great biblical examples of Gideon, Jonathan and Jehosaphat, and he claimed that God would assume the role of battle commander for the Confederacy as he had done for the Israelites in the Old Testament days. Oddly, however, he did not expect supernatural miracles. As did Bishop Elliott, Bunting anticipated a more subtle method of supernatural intervention. He asserted that the Confederacy could not expect miracles, but he stated, "We have the assurance that in answer to prayer, He will, when our cause is just, imbue our leaders with wisdom, make our soldiers courageous and bring victory to our arms and peace to our people. We have no reason for discouragement."[158] Bunting reminded the soldiers that, as with the Israelites of Old Testament times, a nationality could not be created absent from suffering, distress and blood. Bunting encouraged his fellow soldiers to not be dismayed by the immensity of the Northern armies. He maintained that the Confederate soldiers needed only to be faithful to their high calling, and as they were obediently fulfilling their duty with complete dependence on divine aid, the Almighty himself would strike the deathblow to the North.

Bunting even maintained his optimism in July 1863, a time of suffering and discouragement for the Confederacy as a whole following the crushing defeats at Gettysburg and Vicksburg. Bunting still envisioned a great turn in the war that would be brought on by a revival among the troops. He declared:

> But it was for our country we took up arms and turned our backs upon our flowery home, and the sacrifice must be made. To God will we bow. Heaven grant consolation to the many bleeding hearts who bitterly mourn for the missing and the dead, and may God in loving kindness, fill with his presence and love, the vacuums made in our once happy homes. The price of liberty is costly, and yet many more lives must be laid as a sacrifice upon the altar of our young Confederacy, before she is disenthralled from the bondage of the Northmen and has a place and name among the nations of the earth. The costlier our independence, the more it will be appreciated and the heartier our thanks for its blessings. We still hear cheering news of the spiritual condition of the army of Virginia. Her soldiers are pressing into the Kingdom and are enlisting under the banner of the cross. In the Army of Tennessee, there has been much more interest than usual manifested, and the Chaplains at Shelbyville and Tullahoma have held weekly meetings to devise ways and means for the advancement of religion among the troops, and not without encouraging success. We of the cavalry arm of the service, have not the advantage of the infantry, because of our constant duty, our frequent changes of position, and the difficulty of having our regiments together. However, we can but improve our time, when an opportunity presents, and sow the seed in faith. I am enabled now to preach once and twice on every Sabbath, and it is indeed a refreshment for the spirit, when at the bugle's call, we can all assemble in the quiet grove and join in the service of Almighty God. It brings fondly to remembrance the blessing of other and happier days. We know that the loved ones at home do not forget us in their prayers, and this cheers us amid all our fatigues, our perils, and sorrows.[159]

Bunting further noted that in a period of "some weeks," the revival at Tullahoma and Shelbyville, Tennessee, resulted in the conversions of several hundred souls, with many more inquiring about salvation.[160]

Another example of a chaplain and soldier serving without timidity in the Army of Tennessee was Thomas Hopkins Deavenport. Deavenport was born in Pulaski, Tennessee, in 1837. He became a minister for the

Methodist church in Pulaski at the beginning of the Civil War. During the war, Deavenport served as both chaplain and soldier to the Third Tennessee Infantry Regiment. He was captured six times and escaped each time. Following one escape, he went to his home church in Pulaski, Tennessee, to hold a prayer meeting. As he was speaking, someone ran in the church crying, "The Yankees are coming!" He calmly asked the superintendent to come forward, handed him an opened hymnal and climbed the steps to the slaves' gallery and up the trapdoor to the belfry. As he ascended the stairs, the congregation was singing, "Could I but climb when Moses stood and view the landscape o'er."[161] He

This image portrays Reverend R.F. Bunting later in life, many years after the conclusion of hostilities in the Civil War. After the war, he went on to serve as pastor for churches in Nashville, Tennessee; Galveston, Texas; Rome, Georgia and finally, Gallatin, Tennessee, where he died on September 19, 1891. *Courtesy of the Tennessee State Library and Archives.*

spent five days in the church belfry, with two of his cousins supplying him with food and water, hiding from the United States soldiers before returning to his regiment.

Deavenport stated that his decision to join the Confederate army was not made in haste but, rather, followed much contemplation. He recorded in his diary, "A dreadful war having sprung up between the North and South, the North having marshaled their thousands to invade and lay waste our beautiful land, subjugate the people, and rule with a rod of iron. After mature deliberation and much prayer, I felt it to be my duty to give my assistance to the country where I had been nurtured and where the bones of my ancestors reposed."[162] Deavenport contended that he humbled himself before God with all of his heart and sought both God's direction and protection. He further prayed:

If it be thy will, spare me. All I give to thee. Do with me as thou seest best, but whether I live or die, may all be done in the name of the Lord Jesus Christ. If it be necessary that my blood should flow on my country's altar, let it flow, but kind Savior let me dwell in thy presence. Should I fall, let me die at my post, and let my brethren of the Memphis conference know that I fell there, that I died for humanity. Let my sisters know I died to save them from servitude and disgrace. That they may not bow to an unprincipled tyrant.[163]

Deavenport witnessed his congregation doubling as the war progressed. Even through cold and bitter conditions, great numbers of soldiers attended prayer meetings. Deavenport repeatedly wrote of the many souls who were being converted and the many troops that were joining the church. He recorded that most soldiers fasted and attended prayer meetings on the congressionally appointed days for fasting and prayer. Deavenport utilized every opportunity to preach the Gospel and quickly returned to the battlefield upon the conclusion of his sermons. Deavenport wrote in his diary, "It is magnificent to preach to these boys and see them enlisting under the banner of Heaven."[164]

After his capture by the Union army, two Methodist ministers interrogated Deavenport in Chicago as a prisoner of war. The Northern ministers initially asked Deavenport if he were indeed a minister of the Gospel, and he answered in the affirmative. He further admitted that he was a minister with the Methodist Church South in the Conference of Memphis. His interrogators then asked, "Do you in the South regard slavery as a Bible institution?" He answered, "We do."[165] Throughout this meeting, Deavenport further dispelled the commonly held myth that the Christian soldier should not aim his rifle but should instead let God direct the ball. The interrogators questioned whether the reverend participated in the fighting at Donelson, and if so, if he took aim upon firing his rifle. He again answered in the affirmative. The perplexed ministers questioned if it was not considered murder to take aim, and if the proper method for a Christian, especially a minister, was to let God direct the ball. Deavenport responded, "I do not know. I went out to kill."[166]

Although Deavenport believed in the ultimate success of the Confederate cause, he never expected to live to see the consummation of the new government. At times, his writings reflected his mental and physical fatigue and discouragement. In his diary, the reverend often cried out to God questioning how long the war, with all of its suffering, would be allowed to continue, and he pleaded with God for a lasting success and peace. He, however, anticipated his departure prior to the long-sought-after peace. Deavenport wrote, "I think that if faithful for awhile I shall get to Heaven, and mother will be there and it will be home."[167] His greatest desire transformed from a prayer for victory to a cry and a petition for peace and rest. Although Deavenport never lost his faith in the righteousness of the Confederate cause or in the inevitable Confederate victory ahead, the reality of war wore heavy on his mind and body in a manner that the elite civilian clergy could not have related.

Reverend Marcus Bearden DeWitt, DD, was born on March 8, 1835, in Paris, Tennessee. In 1849, he joined the Cumberland Presbyterian Church, and he also attended Cumberland University, from which he graduated in 1859. DeWitt served as the chaplain for the Eighth Tennessee Infantry Regiment, CSA. He described in his diary consistent assembly at prayer meetings throughout the week and public worship on each Sunday when conditions made it possible. DeWitt actively preached, distributed tracts and conducted prayer for the troops. He further described an excellent revival that transpired among the Twenty-third Tennessee Regiment Volunteers, with more than forty conversions in one meeting. DeWitt traveled and preached to other regiments at the request of officers.

The Reverend and Colonel David C. Kelley served as chief of staff to General Nathan Bedford Forrest's command throughout the Civil War. As a Methodist minister, he further served as chaplain to Forrest's cavalry. In this capacity as chaplain, he enjoyed complete freedom to conduct religious services within the camp with the full blessing of Forrest, with whom Kelley established an intimate friendship. Prior to the war, Kelley served as the pastor of a Methodist church in Huntsville, Alabama. Residents described him as a man of education and culture who was greatly admired and beloved.[168] At the beginning of the war, Kelley organized a company of cavalry, and then upon meeting with Forrest's regiment in Memphis, the two commanders merged the units.

Kelley stated of Forrest, "He always gave me the fullest opportunities for preaching in camp, courteously entertaining at his mess-table all preachers whom I might choose to invite. He was always present at such service when it was practicable. While we were messmates there was always family prayer in his tent at night, conducted alternately by the chaplain and myself."[169]

Confederate veteran John Allan Wyeth recounted in his book, *That Devil Forrest: Life of General Nathan Bedford Forrest*, a story from Kelley. The story revolved around a Union chaplain who had been captured by Forrest's men and subsequently made a prisoner of war. The chaplain, understandably, exhibited fear upon learning that his captor was Forrest, but upon entering

The Reverend and Colonel David C. Kelley served as chief of staff to General Nathan Bedford Forrest and was known as the "fighting preacher" among his troops. *Courtesy of the Library of Congress.*

the camp, Forrest invited him to be seated in his headquarters and later invited him to share in their meal. Forrest then beseeched the Union chaplain to ask the blessing over their meal, both startling and confusing the minister, but the Union chaplain readily complied with the request of the general after Forrest assured him that his sentiment was sincere. The following morning, Forrest supplied the chaplain with an escort through Confederate lines, stating that he had no war to make on noncombatants, and he humorously added, "Parson, I would keep you here to preach for me if you were not needed so much more by the sinners on the other side."[170]

Kelley was given the moniker "fighting preacher" by his troops. A captain of an Alabama company described Kelley as "a man of strong character and earnest convictions, who believed so earnestly in the cause of the South that he laid aside his pastoral duties, raised a company of mounted troops, and was now ready to enter the active service of the Confederacy."[171] Sergeant John Johnston, who served under Kelley, recalled, "Colonel Kelley had the confidence of all the soldiers. He was always reliable, gallant, and true, and very popular. Whenever opportunity offered on the Sabbath Day, he would conduct divine services in the camp and sometimes preached to us eloquent sermons out under the shade of the trees."[172] Sergeant Johnston recorded on various occasions that he and the other troops sat on logs awaiting the commencement of the sermon or the administering of the Lord's Supper. Dr. J.B. Cowan explained, "In those days we never started on an expedition but what the men were drawn up in line, and the chaplain, while the heads of all were uncovered, evoked God's blessing on our cause. Nothing called down Forrest's ire quicker or brought surer punishment than for a man to disturb religious service in any part of the camp."[173] During the heated battle for Fort Donelson, Kelley recalled, Forrest rode up to him and exclaimed, "Parson! For God's sake, pray; nothing but God almighty can save that fort!"[174] Through courageous and tenacious fighting, and equally unyielding perseverance in his Christian faith, Kelley encouraged his soldiers both in the Confederate cause and the Christian cause.

Nathan Bedford Forrest is regarded by many military historians as the Civil War's most innovative and successful general, yet his legacy remains as one of the Civil War's most controversial figures. *Courtesy of the Library of Congress.*

Army chaplains played an incredibly significant role in conveying the Confederate as well as the Christian message to their soldiers. The chaplains lived in the harsh world of the army camp and the battlefield. The army chaplain daily faced the same hardships and trials as the soldiers themselves. Yet it was the chaplain's duty to not only remain strong in his personal faith but also to boost the morale and faith of the troops in his care while simultaneously preparing the soldiers for their impending deaths on the battlefield. The success or failure of the Confederacy was often placed on the shoulders of these spiritual guides.

The elite religious leaders, as well as the chaplains, believed that sin—not the Northern army—was destroying the heart and spirit of the cause. Many of the clergy insisted that the early victories created a confidence that led to presumption, which then led to a false security. The soldier then became lax in his duty to God and country. Thus, the nation individually and collectively needed to repent, humble itself before God and beseech Him to once again look upon the Confederacy with His favor. Clergy reminded

The Battle of Fort Donelson was fought from February 11 to February 16, 1862, in Stewart County, Tennessee. The capture of the fort by Union forces opened the Cumberland River as an avenue for the invasion of the South. *Courtesy of the Library of Congress.*

soldiers, "The Israelites were discomfited in battle, were slain by the sword, were visited with pestilence, and were often reduced to very great straits and extremities. Those of whom God intended to make a nation to do His work upon the earth were precisely those whom He tried most severely."[175] To these spiritual guides, victory and independence were not the only purposes in battle. Ministers proposed that God desired to build both character and righteousness in the hearts of the soldiers. It was irrelevant to them if the cause was righteous if the people were not.[176]

Chaplains Quintard, Hogan, Bunting, Deavenport, DeWitt and Kelley were all fervent believers that the Confederate cause was the Christian cause, but they never lost sight of the higher calling of ministering to the souls of the troops. These chaplains filled an enormous void in their regiments through caring for the bodies, minds and spirits of the troops. They were daily examples, living what they preached. Founded on scripture, the message of the army chaplain delivered strength, confidence, consolation, victory and eternal life to the soldiers in the Army of Tennessee, CSA.

CHAPTER 5

SOLDIERS IN THE
ARMY OF TENNESSEE, CSA

Living Sacrifices Freely Given for the Cause

We don't know what is before us today. Our trust is in God.
—Sergeant John Johnston, Army of Tennessee, CSA, April 2, 1865

T he state of Tennessee contributed more than 120,000 men to the
Confederacy and 31,000 men to the Union cause—more than all the
other Confederate states.[177] These ordinary soldiers were much more likely
to hail from a background established and grounded on the family farm than
to have ever received any actual military training or experience. Yet these
ordinary Tennesseans bravely and stubbornly waged the war for four long
and bloody years. Their determination, patriotism and endurance enabled
their cause to continue through the gravest of circumstances. Bishop Stephen
Elliott proudly offered tribute to these soldiers in a sermon on September 18,
1862. He stated:

> *And when we turn to our armies, truly these victories are the victories of the
> privates. God forbid that I should take one atom of honor or of praise from
> those who led our hosts upon those days of glory—from the accomplished
> and skillful Lee—the admirable Crichton of our armies—from the God-
> fearing and indomitable Jackson, upon whose prayer-bedewed banner
> victory seems to wait—from the intrepid Stuart, whose cavalry charges
> imitate those of Murat, from that great host of generals who swarm
> around our country's flag as Napoleon's Marshals did around the Imperial
> Eagle, but nevertheless our victories are the victories of the privates. It is the
> enthusiastic dash of their onsets, the fearless bravery with which they rush*

even to the cannon's mouth, the utter recklessness of life, if so be that its sacrifice may only lead to victory, the heartfelt impression that the cause is the cause of every man, and that success is a necessity. What intense honor do I feel for the private soldier! The officers may have motives other than the cause, the private soldier can have none. He knows that his valor must pass unnoticed, save in the narrow circle of his company; that his sacrifice can bring no honor to his name, no reputation to his family; that if he survives he lives only to enter upon new dangers with the same hopelessness of distinction; that if he dies, he will receive nothing but an unmarked grave, and yet is he proud to do his duty and to maintain his part in the destructive conflict. His comrades fall around him thick and fast, but with a sigh and tear he closes his ranks and presses on to a like destiny. Truly the first monument which our Confederacy rears, when our independence shall have been won, should be a lofty shaft, pure and spotless, bearing this inscription: "TO THE UNKNOWN AND UNRECORDED DEAD."[178]

In the PBS television program *The Civil War*, the late Shelby Foote quoted a Confederate soldier's reply given in response to a question posed to him

George S. Nichols was just sixteen years of age when the Civil War began in 1861. He was a member of the First Tennessee Regiment, CSA, and was a participant in the Battle of Shiloh, where he lost his left eye while engaged with Union forces. Ambrotypes like this first came into use in the early 1850s. Because of their fragility, ambrotypes were held in folding cases. *Courtesy of the Tennessee State Library and Archives.*

by his Union captors. A Union officer asked the Confederate soldier what he was fighting for; the soldier simply replied, "I'm fighting because you all are down here."[179] Individual soldiers expressed many reasons for pursuing the war effort. The traditional concept of Southern honor and duty required one to defend one's home, family, property and land from invasion. Furthermore, Southerners shared a strong belief in individual freedom and individual state sovereignty. Regardless of the diverse reasons that inflamed an individual to rally to the cause, the ordinary soldiers consistently revealed religious themes underlying their rationalizations throughout their diaries, letters and memoirs. Soldiers frequently described their prayers in detail, and they consistently requested prayer from their families and friends in a belief that divine intervention would assure victory.

According to Sidney Romero, the ordinary soldier desired a good preacher in his midst, and there were never enough chaplains.[180] Soldiers, who lived hard lives as farmers, now recognized an immediate need for a supernatural presence larger than themselves. Revivals broke out throughout the Southern army, Bible reading increased and the number of religious conversions grew as carnage and destruction continued to take its toll on the common soldier. The news of an intense religious focus on the part of the Southern armies even reached Washington. President Abraham Lincoln was told, "The rebel soldiers are praying with a great deal more earnestness than our own troops."[181] While the church clergy remained convinced and focused on the victory that God would deliver to them, the soldiers in the fields often simply hoped and prayed that God would deliver them through one more day. The horror of battle, along with the daily deprivations and suffering experienced by the soldier in the field, created a faith that compelled an individual to look intently ahead to preparing one's own soul for an impending death.

James Caswell Edenton, at the age of eighteen, joined the Macon Greys, which was organized on May 27, 1861 into Company B, Thirteenth Regiment of Tennessee Volunteers. Edenton expressed the same fiery religious speech and faith that many Confederate chaplains and officers demonstrated. He praised God for each Southern victory that was accomplished for the Southern army, as well as for each shipment of supplies. Edenton recounted days in which multiple sermons were preached for the soldiers. He attended one prayer service with two hundred fellow soldiers. He regularly prayed for peace and the Lord's protection from the "invading foe." He wrote:

> *Today being Sunday, we heard a sermon from chaplain. He spoke of peace and never before did it fall with such force upon my ears. Would that our*

beloved and happy land might again be restored to peace and quietude. But, if the blood thirsty villains are bent upon controlling this merciless war; then we as the sons of the brave, are willing to contend until it shall have been brought to an end by the great Ruler above. All are resolved to maintain the great principle that was so long cherished by our forefathers. We are fighting for the same principle and God being our helper we will wage as mighty though it cost us seven years toil and hardship and the loss of thousands of the country's best sons.[182]

Edenton asserted that he ended his days by reading from his Bible and then offering thanks and praise for God's guidance and protection.

Terry's Texas Rangers, Eighth Cavalry, fought under the Army of Tennessee, CSA. The cavalry, which organized in Houston on September 9, 1861, with 1,170 men, earned fame throughout the war. Volunteers used their own arms and equipment, and most enlisted for the duration of the war. The cavalry fought under Generals Joseph Wheeler, John Wharton and Nathan Bedford Forrest. They engaged in battles at Shiloh, Murfreesboro

THE

ARMY SONGSTER.

DEDICATED TO THE ARMY OF NORTHERN VIRGINIA.

PUBLISHED BY
GEO. L. BIDGOOD,
RICHMOND, VA.
1864.

The Army Songster, published in 1864, was one of many songbooks carried by soldiers during the Civil War. Religious references are throughout this particular book, including one chorus that reads, "God save the South, Her altars and firesides, God save the South! Now that the war is nigh, Now that we arm to die." *Courtesy of the Center for Popular Music, Middle Tennessee State University.*

and Chickamauga and were part of the Knoxville, Atlanta and Carolina campaigns. On April 26, 1865, the last remaining members of Terry's Texas Rangers, about 30 men, surrendered to Union officers.[183]

One Texas Ranger left a moving account of how his faith influenced his Civil War experience. Private E.H. Ross served in Company A, Eighth Texas Cavalry. On June 28, 1862, just fifteen days prior to his death in Murfreesboro, he wrote his family from Chattanooga: "Tell father and mother not to forget me. Tell them and all the good people of Texas to pray for me and the Southeran Arma [sic] and to pray in earnest and in faith beleaving [sic] that they will receave [sic] what every they ask for or els [sic] I believe we will get whipped after all."[184]

Ross's letters constantly mentioned prayer. Along with his desire for his family and friends to pray for his well-being, he never forgot to remind others to remember "the cause" in their prayers. He envisioned himself accomplishing God's work. On October 22, 1861, he wrote, "Pray for me that I may do my camps duty as a shoulder [sic] of Christ. I am trying to live the life of a Christian tho [sic] I have not seen any religious exercise in line yet. May the Lord bless you and preserve you from all danger and harm that may chance to assail you and if we never meet on this earth a gane [sic] that we may meet in heaven there to compose a family whose separations sorrow and troubles shall forever have an end is my prey [sic]."[185] As the war progressed, Ross recorded more and more religious activities, informing his correspondents of how soldiers benefited from the preaching. He also prayed for the Lord's blessings, guidance and preservation throughout all the trials that lay ahead for the Southern people. Ross returned thanks to God for each day of life and looked solely to God for hope for his future.

Another Army of Tennessee veteran, Sergeant John Johnston, was born on March 11, 1842, just west of Denmark in Madison County, Tennessee. He grew up in a rural environment where "the old Presbyterian Church at Denmark was the religious center of the community."[186] The onset of the Civil War found Johnston in Centre College in Danville, Kentucky, preparing himself to be a Presbyterian minister. With the outbreak of war, however, he surrendered his studies and clerical calling and enlisted in the Confederate army. Johnston enlisted in the Danes, Company K, Sixth Tennessee Infantry, Army of Tennessee, CSA. He later served in Company B, Nixon's Regiment, Tennessee Volunteers. Johnston never returned to the ministry, but nonetheless, he viewed his life as dedicated to the cause of Christ. His writing often showed deep religious convictions. On the day his regiment departed for the war, Reverend David Cochran preached to

Years after the war, John Johnston visited the site of the bloody Battle of Franklin. Johnston's hand-drawn map shows areas where specific skirmishes occurred and where his ancestors lived and their final resting places. *Courtesy of the Tennessee State Library and Archives.*

the regiment. Johnston recalled, "The main point of the sermon was that God directed the minister of death and that we were under His care and protection amidst the dangers of battle as well as at all other times."[187]

Johnston compared the religious nature of the different regiments and camps, as well as the teaching style of the various ministers. He remembered that the Sixth Infantry was refined and religious, while the Seventh Infantry was more profane and wicked. While in winter camp, he recalled erecting a large tent for holding often-impressive religious services. Johnston recounted a familiar scene that occurred just prior to a battle:

> *One day a calvacade* [sic] *composed of Generals Beauregard and Polk and others whom I do not now remember, came riding down our lines accompanied by Reverend Dr. B.M. Palmer, the distinguished Presbyterian preacher from New Orleans. When they reached our part of the line they*

halted and we were assembled near them. Dr. Palmer dismounted, and taking a stump or something else for his pulpit, delivered us an eloquent and stirring address in order to brace us for the coming battle. He was followed by General Polk who was also the Bishop of Louisiana for the Episcopal Church. He, however, sat his horse during his address. Their visit and addresses were enjoyed and appreciated by us. These visits and addresses were made all around the line.[188]

Following victories, Johnston returned thanks to God, whom he credited with delivering victory to the faithful South against the Northern invaders. Following one such victory, Johnston remembered an incident in which fellow soldier Jim Meriwether testified that he could feel his heart just gushing with gratitude and love for God. Religion brought comfort to Johnston in times of defeat as well. Following the Battle of Nashville, when things looked most discouraging, Johnston recalled, "I remember that a young man who sat his horse in front of me and who was a stranger to me expressed his great enjoyment of my singing. After all the hardships and perils of the previous days, I was not despondent but was still able to sing. Besides, I always had an abiding faith in God's providence which sustained and strengthened me under all circumstances."[189]

As the end of the war approached, Johnston fixed his eyes on God and the hope that he found in his faith. He was grateful for God's protection in battle and for the treasured opportunities to return home. He believed that with God nothing was impossible and that God granted mercy to those who trusted in Him. He continued to attend services in camp, often sitting on logs waiting for chaplain D.C. Kelley to preach, and he participated in the Lord's Supper when administered. On April 2, 1865, Johnston wrote in his journal, "We don't know what is before us today. Our trust is in God."[190] On April 3, 1865, Johnston received news of Forrest's defeat. He wrote, "We feel that we are on the eve of a desperate struggle. Many a brave boy must fall before tomorrow's sun is set. Oh God, let Thy presence be with us. Prepare us for all that Thou hast decreed for us, and enable us to do our duty."[191]

The loss of Southern independence did not signal in any way the loss of Johnston's faith. Years after the war, Johnston inscribed on a picture that was placed inside his war memoirs and journal the scripture, "I have been young, and now am old; yet have I not seen the righteous forsaken, nor his seed begging bread."[192]

On September 30, 1861, Colonel James L. Cooper, at the age of seventeen, enlisted with Company C of the Twentieth Tennessee Regiment. He first

John Johnston's faith endured in the years following the end of the Civil War, as witnessed by this note written in his own hand on March 11, 1912, Johnston's seventieth birthday. *Courtesy of the Tennessee State Library and Archives.*

served in Brigadier General Felix K. Zollicoffer's Brigade, then Major General George B. Crittenden's Division and later Major General John C. Breckenridge's Division. Upon entering the army, Cooper joined the temperance order, and he further promised to never touch a card while away from home. On April 13, 1862, he told his father, "I am very well pleased with my mess. They are as moral a mess as any in the 'bull pen.' We do not allow any swearing, vulgar talking or Sabbath-breaking."[193] That same year, while in captivity as a prisoner of war, Cooper stated that captivity improved his morals. He described revivals occurring among the prisoners, with a significant number of converts. He experienced a personal desire to inquire further about religion, although he chose to not actually convert. A fellow prisoner, Pink Martin, introduced "family prayers" in the mess, and the mess continued with them until the prisoners departed for their exchange at Vicksburg.

Although Cooper did not consider himself among the converted, he relied on prayer from others to bring him safely through the war. He also offered prayers up to God on occasion. He stated, "Notwithstanding the fact that I was not much addicted to prayer, a silent petition arose from my heart that God would bring me safely through all my wanderings and dangers back to that home. But other lips and hearts were praying for me and to their intercession, not my own, I owe my safe return. The prayer of the wicked availeth nothing and if there was a wicked, ungrateful wretch in the family, that wretch was myself."[194]

The carnage at the Battle of Stones River in late 1862 led Cooper to write: "Thoughts of home would creep in, and many a fervent prayer was breathed that night by lips, more accustomed to oaths than supplications. Many had gone to eternity that day, all unprepared."[195] Cooper noted the return to the infamous camp sins once the army left the battlefield and reentered the relative safety of camp. In his mind, the wanton sin among the soldiers always overshadowed the periodic revivals. He recorded, "Our camp life was varied by different amusements. For the religiously inclined, there was a considerable revival of religion in the brigade to attract their attention; others not so pious could attend the cockfights, and could also take a hand at poker or seven up. I am afraid those of pious turn of mind were decidedly in the minority."[196]

Cooper did not regard himself as the Christian soldier going off to war, but he did rely on prayer from other Christian soldiers. When writing his memoirs years after the close of the war, the revivals remained in his mind and became a vital part in his record of his life in the Army of Tennessee, CSA.

This lithograph, printed by Middleton, Strobridge & Co. in 1900, shows Union artillery behind infantry lines firing at Confederate troops on the far right during the Battle of Stones River in Murfreesboro, Tennessee. *Courtesy of the Library of Congress.*

Tennessee's most famous Confederate spy is also a good example of the pious nature of many soldiers in the Army of Tennessee. Sam Davis was born on October 6, 1842, in Rutherford County, Tennessee. The Federal army executed him on November 27, 1863, for espionage in Pulaski, Tennessee. Davis gained notoriety and great respect, as later writers deemed him the "Boy Hero of the Confederacy." He became lionized as the ideal Confederate soldier.

Davis left the Nashville Military Academy to enlist in Company I of the First Tennessee Infantry Regiment. In September 1861, Davis and the First Tennessee participated in the Cheat Mountain Campaign in northwest Virginia. Davis followed this campaign with participation in the First Valley Campaign of 1862 under General "Stonewall" Jackson. Davis was given several commendations for his valor and devotion to duty. Upon returning to Tennessee, he fought in the Battle of Shiloh and then received a transfer to Coleman's Scouts.[197]

As a member of Coleman's Scouts in late 1863, Davis failed to successfully perform his final assignment, and Union soldiers captured him. During interrogation, Union General Grenville Dodge warned Davis of the likelihood that he would be found guilty of spying if his case went to trial, and he would then summarily be hanged. Davis replied to the general, "I know, General, I will have to die; but I will not tell where I got the information, and there is no power on earth that can make me tell. You are doing your duty as a soldier, and if I have to die, I shall be doing my duty to God and my country."[198] His final words uttered prior to his execution on November 27, 1863, reportedly were, "I am but a private soldier in the Confederate Army. The man who gave me this information is worth ten thousand more to the Confederate cause than I, and I would sooner die a thousand deaths before I would betray a friend or be false to duty."[199] Davis's death, which stemmed from his uncompromising and determined stance regarding honor and duty both to God and country, assured his place in Confederate memory.

Lieutenant Carrol H. Clark was born on February 26, 1842, in Carthage in Smith County, Tennessee. Prior to the war, he pursued religious studies under the guidance of Reverend Patrick Moore. At the commencement of conflict in Tennessee, Clark resigned from his studies and enlisted in Company I, Sixteenth Tennessee Infantry, under Colonel John Savage.

In 1911, Clark wrote a series of articles based on his wartime diary for the *Spencer Times*, a newspaper located in Spencer, Tennessee. Clark retold his story, beginning with his enlistment serving under Generals Lee and Jackson, two of his favorites, in Virginia. He continued with his long and bloody years serving in Tennessee with other favorite generals such as Generals Leonidas Polk and Nathan Bedford Forrest.

Clark recognized the void that religion filled in the lives of the soldiers and, thus, the place of importance given to religious services and the respect given to religious leaders. He also noted that to outsiders it might have often appeared that the men failed to give proper respect to the clergy and religious services. In one of the articles for the *Spencer Times*, Clark recalled:

> *Parson Dewitt our chaplain, preached for us every Sunday, when we were still. His favorite song was "Jesus Lover of My Soul." You might as well preach to a drove of wild hogs as a lot of soldiers. I have seen boys with blanket spread on the grounds playing cards in a few steps of the preacher while preaching. I think Dewitt was a Presbyterian, and a good man. My recollection is that he continued with us until the end.*[200]

As war casualties mounted, even hardened soldiers gave intense attention to sermons, and the chaplain never lacked converts desiring salvation. Clark told of a time when the chaplains of his brigade decided to hold a religious

This carte-de-visite depicts Lafayette W. Bush in Confederate uniform. Bush was a corporal in the Forty-fourth Tennessee Infantry, CSA. He enlisted on December 30, 1861, in Nashville. His obituary states he professed religion at a soldiers' meeting in New Market Heights, Virginia, in July 1864. Bush died in battle on September 29, 1864, at Fort Harrison, Virginia. *Courtesy of the Tennessee State Library and Archives.*

meeting over a period of several days. They constructed a brush harbor for services. In the middle of services one night, a windstorm snapped a tree, and as the tree fell, it killed three or four of the soldiers. It seemed the soldiers could not escape death, but rather than avoid the services, the incident demonstrated to the soldiers the necessity of preparing for their approaching deaths. Clark, however, avoided the altar calls. He stated, "We were cut off from home and home communication and had not much hope of ever meeting again the loved ones at home. Preachers referred to these facts and had but little trouble in persuading boys to the mourner's bench. I thought of earthly home sweet home and cried, but never went to the mourner's bench, thinking it best to whip the Yanks and then go home."[201]

An example of a Christian soldier who considered it his duty to fight for both family and country and further depended on God for the ultimate defense of his Southern home was found in Captain James J. Womack. Womack was born on July 7, 1834, in Warren County, Tennessee. In civilian life, he was at various times a farmer, a lawyer and a newspaper publisher. Womack enlisted in Company E, Sixteenth Regiment Tennessee Volunteers, which was formed almost completely of Warren County men. In his diary, Womack described the founding of and purpose of Company E. He wrote:

> Twelve months ago today I left my happy and prosperous home in McMinnville, Tennessee, to battle for my country's freedom and Independence, which were then denied her, and still are, by a vaunting and insulting enemy. In consequence of the odious and intolerable tyranny and duplicity beginning to be forced on the people of that, and other states, I felt it to be my duty not only to my country, but also to myself and family, to enlist in the C.S. army. So regarding it, I was instrumental in organizing the first Company raised in my county, styled "The Warren Guards" (a title of my own selection) which has twice honored me with its Captaincy, and upon whose gallantry I fully rely, and of whose members its friends will in a coming day be proud. During the year we have undergone many privations and hardships; especially was the fall and winter campaign among the mountains in western Va. severe. Here we were frequently deprived of even the few comforts that the soldier in the field might reasonable expect, having to sleep on the cold, wet and sometimes frozen ground, with no other covering than the canopy of Heaven. Day after day we marched over muddy roads and snow covered mountains, sometimes barefoot and

almost without clothing. Notwithstanding all this, and notwithstanding the clouds of war grow thicker and darker still, yet we have never seen the hour when we would give up the struggle for Southern Independence. And we never will, but by the help of God, Liberty and Independence will yet be ours.[202]

Bible reading, prayer time and attendance at religious services were of the highest importance to Womack throughout his enlistment. When in camp, he daily recorded Bible passages and particular prayers in his diary. He further described religious services, the chaplains and the different ministers who were available to preach to the men. He often recorded hearing more than one sermon a day. He further noted times when the soldiers were presented with testaments and religious tracts. Womack was especially pleased to note the times when the soldiers were given an opportunity to partake of the communion service while in the field. He also recorded the deaths of certain members of his company and stated that these men died in the faith.

Womack, however, was disgusted by the apparent lack of respect among officers for the Sabbath day. He complained, "I am shocked to see such a total disregard for the Holy Sabbath. Commanders of the army may excuse themselves for thus occupying the holy hours given for man's rest and devotion to God, but I do not conclude the Great Ruler of battles will. Six days He has given, in which man is to labor, and on the seventh, which is the Lord's Day, he is to rest. This is the first Sabbath I have entirely neglected my Bible in many months."[203] Regardless of the failures of the commanders in conducting themselves as soldiers of the cross, Womack always maintained his faith that "the God of Battles will never forsake a people battling for right and justice."[204]

William A. Brown enlisted in Stanford's Battery of Light Artillery in Grenada, Mississippi. Following the war, on December 21, 1867, he began compiling what he described as an "exact transcript" from a "notebook" that he maintained most of the time he served with the Confederate army. At the beginning of the war, he discovered himself involved in an atmosphere that most closely resembled an exciting adventure, but with the onset of actual battles, instead of small skirmishes, his attitude and those of his compatriots in camp drastically changed. He declared, "Things began to look serious and it was evident a battle was before us and no longer a jesting matter. Orders were sent around for us to keep quiet—the enemy being a short distance in front. Quietly, almost silently, we returned to rest and thoughts of the morrow. Many a whispered prayer was uttered that night, no doubt by lips unaccustomed to prayer."[205]

Throughout his notebook, Brown described his attendance at church services. He even noted the times when he missed church and the days with more than one service offered for the soldier to attend. Brown supplied an example of the wartime importance of attending religious services and the equal unimportance of seeking out one's individual denomination, a choice that prior to the war was very uncommon. Brown recalled battery officers accompanying him to attend services at Baptist, Methodist and even Catholic churches. Brown noted the successful revivals and his attendance at them throughout his notebook, stating the periods of time when "church still holds every night."[206] He further described the very cold conditions that the soldiers would endure to attend services, and often ministers baptized converts in such conditions. Brown believed that religion flourished throughout the war years, as documented by the tremendous crowds found within the churches. While visiting a very crowded Catholic church in Dalton, Georgia, he had no choice but to enter through a window.

Brown, regardless of his faith, at times demonstrated a cynical view of religion in the army. After witnessing an execution, Brown wrote, "Some of our boys witnessed the execution. The crime of these men was desertion—going home, perhaps, to see their wives and little ones without permission, but such are the regulations of a Christian Army."[207] Yet Christianity offered hope to Brown and his fellow soldiers. On August 14, 1864, Brown and a Lieutenant Scott visited a church in Atlanta. As they listened to the sermon, the church windows rattled with the roar of artillery. The louder the cannons raged and the more death and destruction that visited the armies, the more critical simple sermons and Bible reading became to men such as Brown.

Private J.W. Harmon enlisted in the Thirty-fifth Regiment Alabama Infantry, which fought with the Army of Tennessee. In accounting his reasons for joining the Confederacy, he declared, "I felt it a duty to obey and contribute my humble efforts in serving the cause which every true Southern man held as just and sacred."[208] He described the day of his enlistment in his diary, stating that the local Presbyterian church held a service for the soldiers going to war, and following the sermon, each soldier was presented with a Bible.

Harmon praised God for blessing him with health and protecting him through dangers so that he could be part of the "glorious struggle." He pointed to the magnificent religious work occurring in the army to illustrate the presence of God. At one campsite, Harmon recorded:

J.W. Harmon's school, LaGrange Military Academy. *Courtesy of the Tennessee State Library and Archives.*

We had a nice location for camping, being situated near a clear and rippling stream of water; on the whole it might be said our stay there was a pleasant treat to, [sic] for the Chaplains held religious services, and a good spiritual meeting was soon in progress. Many enjoyed from two to three good sermons each day, and there were quite a number of conversions. This certainly was a feast for the souls of poor soldiers, and it was very seldom we had such opportunities of a religious nature.[209]

Soon after the Battle of Franklin, Union troops captured Harmon, who sat in prison until the war was over. He still rejoiced in the blessings of God, thanking the Lord for sparing his life, protecting him through all dangers and guiding his steps. He pledged to fulfill some religious mission with the life that Providence had spared. For all of his gratefulness, however, he recalled his disappointment in the lack of Christianity demonstrated to him by his Union prison guards. He declared:

It matters not which side men were made prisoners of war, whenever they were treated cruelly and starved, the perpetrators of such acts were no better than barbarians, and devoid of those tender feelings of pity and charity which should predominate within the hearts of all men who claim to possess the great principles that are taught by Christianity, and to which civilization and Enlightenment should point them to. A Christian people—it matters not where found—should ever act as becometh their pretensions and though there may be differences in beliefs and principles, even when arms may have to be resorted to, still Christianity should shine forth to illuminate all the dark clouds that overhang human life.[210]

After the Confederacy experienced defeat and the soldiers surrendered their arms and journeyed home to attempt to reconstruct their lives, Harmon, like so many others, looked to religion to explain their horrible and costly loss. His strength and security came from his ability to "trust to an all-wise Providence, who does all things well to guide in that way which would result in the most good."[211] Although he could not explain the reasons behind God's actions, he strongly argued that the Lord only did what was right, and thus, He could not be questioned. Harmon summed up these feelings in the beginning of his memoirs. He wrote, "An all wise Providence saw fit that things should be changed from what was so earnestly designed, and we have bowed with reverence to His will."[212]

Sam Watkins was born on June 26, 1839, near Columbia, Tennessee. He attended Jackson College in Columbia. When he was twenty-one years of age, he enlisted in the Bigby Grays on April 20, 1861, and later in the Maury Grays on May 15, 1861. The latter group was organized as Company H of the First Tennessee Infantry Regiment.[213] Watkins first fought as part of the Army of Northern Virginia, and he later fought throughout

J.W. Harmon's letter, "A Narrative from an Old Confederate." *Courtesy of the Tennessee State Library and Archives.*

94

most all of the major Tennessee campaigns. He was wounded three times. Bishop Charles Quintard was the chaplain for the First Tennessee Regiment.

Watkins wrote one of the most famous soldier memoirs, *Company Aytch: A Side Show of the Big Show*. He presented his sincere faith while acknowledging the hypocrisy of some chaplains who refused to fight alongside the infantry. He remembered one Sabbath when the soldiers were drawn together to listen to a sermon from a preacher from Nashville. The army was prepared and especially anxious for the service because they expected to go into battle sometime in the next couple of days. Watkins recalled this preacher was one of the "big ones," and this added to the desire on the part of the soldiers to hear the sermon. As the chaplain traveled with the brigade, he encouraged the men to be brave and kill, and he contended that he would gladly fight alongside them. As the Battle of Chickamauga began, Watkins recalled, "The Reverend L.L.D. stops to listen like a old sow when she hears the wind, and says, 'Remember, boys, that he who is killed will sup to-night in Paradise.' Some soldier hallooed at the top of his voice, 'Well, Parson, you come along and take supper with us.' Boom! Whir! A bomb blast and the parson at that moment put spurs to his horse and was seen to limber to the rear, and almost every soldier yelled out, 'The parson isn't hungry, and never eats supper.'"[214]

Watkins also recounted the respect he had for others who remained with the soldiers throughout the war. He believed the spirits of the slain soldiers traveled with the men of the company even while their souls were safe with God. Watkins recalled camp preachers, remembering specific sermons. He broke, however, with the popular Confederate translation of the conflict by consistently referring to the war as "unholy and uncalled for." Yet following this description, he confirmed his belief that "He that ruleth the heavens doeth all things well."[215] Watkins carried a Bible in his side pocket when in the service, and at the Battle of Cat Creek, a Minié ball passed through his Bible. Watkins acknowledged his gratitude for knowing God, and he fully expected to see his fallen comrades again in heaven. He stated that the chaplains held divine service on the Sabbath and always offered prayer in the evenings at retreat. It was his belief that these prayers and services greatly improved the morale of the army.

Watkins recounted a time in the winter of 1863–64 in Dalton, Georgia, when a revival began, with religious services every day and night. During this period, soldiers seriously contemplated the conditions of their souls, and thus, they turned out in great numbers to attend the services. The chaplains had placed a long mourners' bench in front of the soldiers for the repentant sinners to use. As ten soldiers were kneeling, a tree that had been smoldering for days fell across the mourners' bench, killing all ten of the soldiers. As in the similar scenario that occurred in Lieutenant Clark's regiment, this tragic event did not discourage attendance at services. In reacting to this shocking and deadly accident, Watkins concluded, "God had heard their prayers. Their souls had been carried to Heaven. Hereafter, henceforth, and forevermore, there was no more marching, battling, or camp duty for them. They had joined the army of the hosts of Heaven."[216]

Watkins also recalled in his memoirs the song and prayer book published by Bishop Quintard. He claimed to have memorized the song and prayer book by heart, and twenty years after the close of the war, he still possessed a copy of it. Quintard left an enduring impression on Watkins, who believed that Quintard's very nature was one of love. He stated, "He loved the soldiers, and the soldiers loved him, and deep down in his heart of hearts was a deep and lasting love for Jesus Christ, the Redeemer of the world, implanted there by God the Father Himself."[217]

Watkins further mourned the loss of General and Bishop Leonidas Polk. Watkins remembered, "Every private soldier loved him."[218] He recalled that the soldiers always referred to the general as "Bishop" and that he had always maintained the respect, honor and love of all the soldiers. Throughout the war, Watkins experienced the loss of a multitude of friends and acquaintances. M. Thomas Inge, editor of *Company Aytch: Or a Side Show of the Big Show*, discovered, "Out of the 120 men who enlisted with Watkins in Company H in 1861, he was one of only seven survivors."[219]

Numerous diaries written by private soldiers in the Army of Tennessee, CSA, exist in incomplete forms. Many soldiers never lived to complete their wartime diaries, and others found little time in the madness and mayhem of army service to maintain a commitment to writing the events of their daily lives. Nonetheless, even in diaries that exist only in the barest form, the importance these soldiers placed on religion and their spiritual views regarding the conflict were often passionately expressed.

Private Stephen A. Jordan enlisted in Biffle's Ninth Regiment, Tennessee Cavalry, from 1862 to 1865. He later joined the cavalry brigade of General Forrest. In a diary entry common to his overall diary writings, he stated, "I thank God that I am still permitted to live and see another birthday," and on yet another occasion, "Had a big fight. Drove the Yankees five miles…I came very near being captured and killed, but I thank God I made my escape."[220] Jordan regularly praised God for protecting him during each battle. He further found it important to note, in his often extremely succinct writings, the services and sermons preached to the soldiers.

Colonel Frank W. McNairy was killed in the Second Battle of Fort Donelson on February 3, 1863, when 2,500 Confederate troops under Major General Joseph Wheeler attacked a small garrison at Dover, Tennessee, under Colonel A.C. Harding. The Confederate failure to capture the garrison left Federals in control of Middle Tennessee. Nathan Bedford Forrest denounced Wheeler after this battle and refused to serve under him again. *Courtesy of the Tennessee State Library and Archives.*

Joseph R. Mothershead of Haynesville, Missouri, maintained a concise journal throughout the war until his death on August 6, 1864, in Atlanta. G.W. Rogers was the chaplain to his regiment, and Private Mothershead also recalled hearing sermons in the camps. He stated in February 1862 that prayer meetings were held in the regiment every night. Mothershead believed in the sacred nature of the Confederate cause, and he, like many others, pointed to the deeds of General "Stonewall" Jackson to demonstrate that God considered the Confederate cause just, given Jackson's apparent invincibility. In consideration of possible aid arriving from Europe, on June 10, 1862, Mothershead proclaimed, "It behooves us as a people struggling for the rights of liberty to put our reliance in our own arms aided by that Divine Power that never fails to set on the side of justice and right."[221]

Private William Mebane Pollard enlisted in Company D, First Tennessee Regiment, also known as the Williamson Grays. He initially fought under General "Stonewall" Jackson before returning to carry on the struggle in Tennessee. Each week, Pollard commented in his journal regarding his attendance at religious services. He wrote of attending church whenever possible and recounted sermons that especially ministered to him. On March 16, 1862, a group of women impressed him by holding up flags inscribed with the words "God is for us" as the army marched by.[222]

Other soldiers, although maintaining faith in the sacredness of the cause, nonetheless hoped for a sign from the God of Battles to demonstrate that He indeed was with them. James Brickell Murfree enlisted in Company I, First Tennessee Regiment, and state officials designated him assistant surgeon on June 9, 1861. While in Holston Hospital in New Market, Tennessee, on June 5, 1863, Dr. Murfree received a letter from Chas R. Donoho. Donoho remarked: "If our cause is triumphant at Vicksburg, I will more firmly believe that it is favored by Him who led the Jews out of captivity. My prayer is that the whole host of Lincoln may be swept from the face of the earth soul and body. Is not that more generous than David was towards his enemy? Let death seize upon them, and let them go down quick into hell: for wickedness is in their dwellings and among them."[223] The biblical choice of using David for an example mirrored the image that the Confederate government and elite clergy had earlier promoted. The illustration once again pitted David at war with Goliath, and as the above writer suggested, the Confederacy hoped to remove the head of Goliath quickly.

Henry Melville Doak was born on August 3, 1841, in Washington County, Tennessee. Although he believed that slavery had been an effective tool throughout history to elevate the "downtrodden," at the time of the Civil War, he believed that slavery had served its purpose in America and needed to end. Doak, however, was an ardent proponent for secession from the North. Following the fall of Fort Sumter into Confederate hands, Doak joined the Knoxville Guards. While visiting Charleston, Private Doak enjoyed seeing the first submarines that were being constructed for the Confederate States of America. He viewed both the *Hunley* and the *David*. Private Doak surmised that the *David* was thusly named because of "the damage it was expected to do the Federal Goliath."[224] Later, while in a Union prison, Doak recalled both the piety and wickedness in existence among the prisoners. Prayer meetings transpired concurrently with gaming opportunities. Doak resisted both the "sinful" acts and joining the prayer meetings, preferring instead to conduct his prayers in private.

Henry Melville Doak, shown here in his Confederate Marine uniform, joined Company E, Nineteenth Tennessee (the Knoxville Guards), following the fall of Fort Sumter into Confederate hands. After the war, Doak became a lawyer, educator and journalist, ultimately owning the *Nashville Banner* newspaper. *Courtesy of the Tennessee State Library and Archives.*

Countless soldiers only left brief mentions about the everyday events of army life. Private F.J. Paine inscribed in his diary, "G.W. Calahan has the appointment of Chaplain now in our command and is taking a good deal of interest in it. He has a revival now going on. Has had a few professions, and quite a number at the anxious seat, several others of the same company. And they all seem to be very much affected and I think they are really in earnest."[225]

Similarly, Private Andrew Rice, concerned over the wickedness he found in the army camps, drew encouragement from the successful revivals occurring within the brigade. Although he and his regiment had been denied religious services since separating from their brigade, which he claimed made their days dull, he wrote of the services occurring elsewhere. Rice observed, "There is a big protracted meeting going on in our brigade and has been for over two months. There has been a good many conversions. I don't know how long it will go on, but I am in hopes that it will be a general thing throughout the army."[226]

Private William J. Rogers of the Thirteenth Infantry Tennessee Volunteers maintained a diary between June 1862 and May 1863. Rogers regularly entered his attendance at camp religious services, as well as those services that he traveled several miles to attend. On May 10, 1863, Rogers wrote in his diary that a "grand revival is going on in the Twelfth Tennessee Regiment. Eight converts were baptized in Duck River at two o'clock, P.M."[227] Rogers, however, did not necessarily believe that the camp atmosphere was the most conducive to promoting religious worship. On at least one occasion, he noted the ignorance of the preacher, and at other times, he longed for the spiritual ways of the past. On March 16, 1863, Rogers wrote, "Oh! that I was a boy once more at home in peace and knew nothing of the horrors of war. Then I would serve my parents, my country; yes, my God. Though it is my duty here, but I have often thought a soldier has no time to serve any but Generals and President Davis."[228] Ironically, a few days thereafter, on March 27, 1863, Rogers noted in his diary the day set apart by President Davis as a day of thanksgiving and prayer for all of the Confederate people.

As a result of the many defeats they suffered, Tennessee soldiers accepted that their losses may have been a chastisement or possible abandonment by God. Many soldiers understood why: there was sin in the camp. Joseph Anderson Rogers served as the hospital steward for Wright's Brigade, Cheatham's Division, in General Polk's Corps. In 1864, he summed up the woeful state of the Army of Tennessee: "Most of the men have testaments and packs of cards in their pockets."[229] The clergy and many private soldiers argued that it was this lack of complete surrender and dedication to the God of Battles that contributed to disaster upon disaster. When writing his parents about the death of his brother, Private William H. Sugg stated, "We should bear this our affliction with as much fortitude as we can and say with Job, the Lord giveth and the Lord taketh away and this the scriptures tell us in another place, whom the Lord loveth he also chasteneth. Who knows but this is a chastisement sent upon us."[230] Private Thomas R. Hooper of Company A, Sixteenth Tennessee Infantry, appealed to the mercy of a just God. On December 28, 1862, before the Battle of Stones River, he entered a simple statement and plea in his diary: "God help us for we are sinners. Help, help us."[231] Throughout his diary, Private Hooper sought the aid of God and requested his blessings on his family and friends.

Regardless of wins or losses, many soldiers fixed their eyes on their Savior, who was their source for strength and help, and determined to give all for the cause. After the bloodbath at Shiloh, W.H. Williams wrote his wife on May 19, 1862: "I shall put my trust in God and do the best I can."[232] Their Confederate leaders emphatically supported their faith and promoted a holy Christian cause. R.W. Banks served as sergeant major to the Thirty-seventh Mississippi Infantry in Cantey's Brigade, General Polk's Corps. In his memoirs, he included a general order written from Cassville, Georgia, on May 19, 1864, by General Joseph Johnston. The general declared, "We may confidently trust that the Almighty Father will still reward the patriot's toils and bless the patriot's banners."[233] Banks recalled a Private W. Peacock of Company G who had participated in the fighting at the Battle of Franklin. He proposed, "The God of Battles, it seems to me, extended His special providence to this brave man, and thus made possible his escape unharmed from the Sheol of shot and shell through which he went on that dread day."[234] Even following what would more accurately be described as a massacre than a battle, soldiers still believed they experienced the hand of God on themselves and their country and maintained hope that in the end, God would bring them a decisive victory.

At other times, death, and not an escape from it, drew the attention of the soldiers to matters eternal. Lieutenant Edwin H. Rennolds of Company K, Fifth Tennessee Infantry, described a death scene that occurred at the Battle of Resaca, Georgia. He wrote:

> *Captain J.B. Ward, Company K, was killed, and also Corporal A.D. Beckwith of Company D. He had been a very wicked man, but was converted at the Dalton revival a few weeks previous. He was sitting by a small hickory, too small to protect him, and when struck by a Minnie ball, seemed to realize that the end was nigh. He dropped his gun, commenced to clap his hands, and exclaimed: "Bless the Lord!" and in a few seconds was dead. This scene affected all who witnessed it, and one comrade tells me that it changed the whole current of his life.*[235]

Alexis de Tocqueville, in his observations of mid-nineteenth-century America, claimed there was "no country in the world where the Christian religion retained a greater influence over the souls of men than in America."[236] Confederate private George Thompson Blakemore summed up the prayers of the soldiers in the Army of Tennessee, CSA. He proclaimed, "May God be my guide in serving my country. Let the times and the excitement be as they may, the God of Heaven be with the Southern people and Southern army."[237]

As defeats visited the armies, soldiers and ministers alike sought answers to explain why their God had withdrawn his hand of blessing. Civilian ministers and the women and men at home complained, in explanation for the tragic turn of events, that the sin in the camps invited the wrath of God. The soldiers, on the other hand, argued that the sins committed by the people behind the lines brought defeat. The ministers proclaimed that the soldiers were indeed provoking God to anger with their card playing, drinking and swearing, thereby forcing the Holy Lord to hide His face from their just and right cause. They complained that Confederates were allowing their selfish flesh with its vanity, pride, ambition and evil to rule over their godly spirits. Ministers and soldiers alike argued that the political situation had progressed to a point where, without victory, there would only be unconditional surrender. Chaplains explained to their comrades that surrender would not be to Christians like themselves but, rather, to a party of infidels. Although there was no doubt among most Confederates of the sacredness of their cause, even the private soldiers recognized that the army needed to repent and fully rely on the mercy of God in order to truly become a sacred people within a sacred nation.

Until the very end, surprisingly large numbers of Southerners refused to believe that God had abandoned their cause. They remained convinced that He would deliver a last-minute victory against all odds.[238] The Old Testament supplied numerous examples of times when God intervened miraculously near the very end for His people of Israel. Confederates acknowledged that God might severely try them and even chastise them for their sins, as He did so often with ancient Israel, but in the end He would save His people from defeat. Following defeat, some Confederate soldiers held on to the belief that within the next generation, God would yet grant independence to the South. The message of the holy cause had been preached with such grand fervor that it was extremely difficult for Confederates to accept that they had been in error all along and that God had not sanctioned their cause.

Chapter 6

Conclusion

Both read the same Bible, and pray to the same God; and each invokes His aid against the other. The prayers of both could not be answered—that of neither has been answered fully.
—President Abraham Lincoln, Second Inaugural, March 4, 1865

Historian James McPherson concluded, "Civil War armies were, arguably, the most religious in American History."[239] Years earlier, Sidney Romero claimed an even stronger position by maintaining that if deep religious sentiments could have won a war, the South could not have been defeated.[240] Religion laid the foundation upon which Southern nationalism was built, unified people from different backgrounds and classes and provided a spiritual reason for the yeoman farmer to fight in a war driven by the issue of slavery. Politicians, generals, bishops, chaplains and common soldiers alike constantly spoke of their faith, their existence in the will of God, the sacred nature of the Confederate defensive war, their total dependence on God and the certainty that God would deliver complete victory to His Southern people. In defeat, these Confederates repented for their sins, which they believed alone destroyed the holy cause.

There is little doubt that certain Confederate leaders took advantage of the sincere abiding faith of so many and misused their power in order to propagandize the need and reasons for war. Additionally, not all of those living during this time of renewed and impassioned faith and revival agreed with those popular sentiments being espoused from the clergy and political leaders. Novelist Mark Twain served in the Confederate army for a term of about two weeks and then deserted and ventured west. Twain reached a caustic conclusion regarding both Union and Confederate armies who, grounded on the foundation of the Bible and religion, rationalized and justified the killing of thousands of their fellow countrymen. He entitled his vision of the religious state of affairs existing in the nation as "The War Prayer." He wrote:

> *O Lord our God, help us to tear (enemy) soldiers to bloody shreds with our shells; help us to cover their smiling fields with the pale forms of their patriot dead; help us to drown the thunder of the guns with the shrieks of their wounded writhing in pain; help us to lay waste their humble homes with a hurricane of fire; help us to wring the hearts of their unoffending widows with unavailing grief; help us to turn them out roofless with their little children to wander unfriended the wastes of their desolated land in rags and hunger and thirst. We ask it in the spirit of love, of him who is the Source of Love, and who is the ever-faithful refuge and friend of all that are sore beset and seek His aid with humble and contrite hearts.* [241]

In 1861, Samuel Langhorne Clemens, aka Mark Twain, enlisted in the Confederate militia but deserted a mere two weeks later. In his 1883 memoir, *Life on the Mississippi*, Twain wrote, "In the South the war is what A.D. is elsewhere; they date from it." *Courtesy of the Library of Congress.*

Conclusion

Although Mark Twain painted a cynical picture of current events, common soldiers nonetheless left for battle believing God and justice were on their side. Religion existed as a central force in America's identity, and thus, the Southerners used religion to survive and interpret the war and to build new lives after the war ended.[242]

Prior to the Civil War, decades of evangelizing had prepared the South for a holy war. Denominational splits between the North and the South foretold events long before the government splintered. Southern culture had long connected Christianity with the concerns of daily living, including slavery, femininity and the role of the Southern gentleman. When Union troops invaded Southern land, there was no question in the minds of the majority that a defensive war to protect one's home and family was just. Early victories and great revivals seemed to provide evidence that the Almighty was indeed with the Confederate army. As the war wore on, prayer, and the gifts of peace and hope that accompanied it, became ever more important. The Army of Tennessee saw many defeats—Fort Donelson, Nashville, Shiloh, Chattanooga and Franklin, to name a few. Confederates needed religion in their most trying hour, and they clung to their faith even after all appeared to be lost. As good disciples, they accepted the blame for their defeats, acknowledging their sins, and they continued to bless God, who, as so many soldiers had written in their diaries, always does that which is right. God had proven to these men serving in the Army of Tennessee that He was truly their "refuge and strength, a very present help in trouble."[243]

NOTES

ACKNOWLEDGEMENTS

1. Rable, *God's Almost Chosen Peoples*, 7.

CHAPTER 1

2. The Army of Tennessee, CSA, was formed on November 20, 1862, renaming the Army of Mississippi. As the Army of Mississippi, it had fought the Battles of Shiloh and Perryville.
3. Miller, Stout and Wilson, *Religion and the American Civil War*, 4.
4. Silver, *Confederate Morale*, 101.
5. Ibid., 57.
6. Ibid., 93.
7. Norton, *Rebel Religion*, 114.
8. Romero, *Religion in the Rebel Ranks*, 4.
9. Ibid., 70.
10. Ibid., 128.
11. Genovese, *A Consuming Fire*.
12. Ibid., 71.
13. Gilpin-Faust, *Creation of Confederate Nationalism*, 22.
14. Ibid., 22.
15. Miller, Stout and Wilson, *Religion and the American Civil War*, 5.

16. Harry S. Stout and Christopher Grasso, "Civil War, Religion, and Communications: The Case of Richmond," in *Religion and the American Civil War*, ed. Miller, Stout and Wilson, 318.

17. Ibid., 320. See also Preamble to the Constitution of the Confederate States, March 11, 1861.

18. Eugene D. Genovese, "Religion in the Collapse of the American Union," in *Religion and the American Civil War*, ed. Miller, Stout and Wilson, 74.

19. Phillip Shaw Paludan, "Religion and the American Civil War," in *Religion and the American Civil War*, ed. Miller, Stout and Wilson, 22.

20. Mark A. Noll, "The Bible and Slavery," in *Religion and the American Civil War*, ed. Miller, Stout and Wilson, 43.

21. Paludan, "Religion and the American Civil War," 28.

22. James M. McPherson, "Afterword," in *Religion and the American Civil War*, ed. Miller, Stout and Wilson, 410.

23. Stout and Grasso, "Civil War, Religion, and Communications," 343.

24. Kurt O. Berends, "Wholesome Reading Purifies and Elevates the Man: The Religious Military Press in the Confederacy," in *Religion and the American Civil War*, ed. Miller, Stout and Wilson, 141.

25. Stout and Grasso, "Civil War, Religion, and Communications," 326.

26. Bertram Wyatt-Brown, "Church, Honor, and Secession," in *Religion and the American Civil War*, ed. Miller, Stout and Wilson, 101.

27. Ibid., 103.

28. Chesebrough, *God Ordained This War*, 5.

29. Berends, "Wholesome Reading," 146.

30. Gilpin-Faust, *Creation of Confederate Nationalism*, 22.

31. Charles Reagan Wilson, "Religion and the American Civil War in Comparative Perspective," in *Religion and the American Civil War*, ed. Miller, Stout and Wilson, 395.

32. Stout and Grasso, "Civil War, Religion, and Communications," 333.

33. Boles, *Irony of Southern Religion*, 75.

34. Stout and Grasso, "Civil War, Religion, and Communications," 319.

Chapter 2

35. Boles, *Irony of Southern Religion*, 35.

36. Davis, "Farewell to the United States Senate," 221–25.

37. Davis, "Inaugural Address," 1:64–66, as reprinted in Crist and Dix, eds., *The Papers of Jefferson Davis*, 7:46–50.

38. Ibid.
39. Ibid.
40. Ibid.
41. Davis, "Speech at Richmond."
42. Gilpin-Faust, *Creation of Confederate Nationalism*, 26.
43. Stout and Grasso, "Civil War, Religion, and Communications," 320.
44. Stephen Elliott, *Ezra's Dilemma*, A Sermon Preached in Christ Church Savannah, Friday August 21, 1863, Being the Day of Humiliation, Fasting, and Prayer, Appointed by the President of the Confederate States, Savannah, GA: Power Press of George N. Nichols, 1863, Papers of Stephen Elliott. University Archives and Special Collections, The University of the South, Sewanee, Tennessee, 1, 6, Scripture taken from the Bible, Ez. 8:22.
45. Fellman, *Making of Robert E. Lee*, 88.
46. Romero, *Religion in the Rebel Ranks*, 86.
47. Davis, Pohanka and Troiani, "Robert E. Lee," in *Civil War Journal*, 149.
48. Robertson, *Stonewall Jackson*, ix.
49. Taylor, *Destruction and Reconstruction*, 170.
50. Smith, Letter on the Death of Stonewall Jackson, May 11, 1863.
51. Robertson, *Stonewall Jackson*, x.
52. Jackson, Letter to Sister Laura, Lexington, Virginia, November 14, 1854, Stonewall Jackson Papers.
53. Robertson, *Stonewall Jackson*, xii–xiii.
54. Ibid.
55. Ewell, *The Making of a Soldier*, 170.
56. Robertson, *Stonewall Jackson*, xv.
57. Ibid., xviii.
58. Thomas Jonathan Jackson, Letter to Rev. (Dr.) Francis McFarland, Augusta County, Virginia, July 31, 1862, Stonewall Jackson Papers.
59. Fulkerson, Letter to Wife, Selina, Regarding the Death of Stonewall Jackson, May 18, 1863, Fulkerson Family Papers.
60. Smith, General Order No. 30, May 13, 1863.
61. Daniel W. Stowell, "Stonewall Jackson and the Providence of God," in *Religion and the American Civil War*, ed. Miller, Stout and Wilson, 196.
62. Miller, Stout and Wilson, *Religion and the American Civil War*, 10.
63. Robertson, *Stonewall Jackson*, ix.
64. Leonidas Polk, Reel 1, 44020, RG 39:32, Box 89C, Polk Papers.
65. Ibid., Leonidas Polk to Stephen Elliott, January 31, 1857.
66. Ibid., Stephen Elliott to Leonidas Polk, August 6, 1861.
67. Ibid.

68. Leonidas Polk, Tennessee State Library and Archives, *Civil War Collection (1861–1865)*, Mf.Ac.No.824, Diaries, Reel 4, Box 11, Folder 7.

69. Leonidas Polk, General Orders No. 1, Head Quarters, Meridian, Mississippi, December 23rd 1863, Lieut. General Commanding Leonidas Polk, Box 39:31, Folder 34, September–December 1863, Polk Papers.

70. Leonidas Polk to Lilly Polk, June 1, 1864, Box 39:31, Folder 36A, June–July 1864, Polk Papers.

71. General Joseph E. Johnston, Box 39:31, Folder 36A, June–July 1864, Polk Papers.

72. Elliott, *Funeral Services at the Burial of the Right Rev. Leonidas Polk, DD*, St. Paul's Church, Augusta, Georgia, June 29, 1864. Papers of Stephen Elliott, 9.

73. Ibid.

74. Ibid., 10.

75. Ibid., 15.

76. Ibid., 14.

77. Sarah Dorsey to Leonidas Polk, February 20, 1862, Private Collection, Box 39:31, Folder 30, January–March 1862, Polk Papers.

78. Ayers, "A Review of Randall M. Miller, Harry S. Stout, and Charles Reagan Wilson."

Chapter 3

79. Romero, *Religion in the Rebel Ranks*, 105, 94.

80. McMillan, *Alabama Confederate Reader*, 96.

81. Ibid., 96–97.

82. Miller, Stout and Wilson, *Religion and the American Civil War*, 5.

83. Kurt O. Berends, "Wholesome Reading Purifies and Elevates the Man: The Religious Military Press in the Confederacy," in *Religion and the American Civil War*, ed. Miller, Stout and Wilson, 9.

84. Mark A. Noll, "The Bible and Slavery," in *Religion and the American Civil War*, ed. Miller, Stout and Wilson, 48.

85. Berends, "Wholesome Reading Purifies," 135.

86. Gilpin-Faust, *Creation of Confederate Nationalism*, 82.

87. Ibid., 23, citing *Religious Herald*, January 1, 1863. Also Silver, *Confederate Morale*, 58.

88. Stephen Elliott, *Address of the Rt. Rev. Stephen Elliott, D.D. to the 39th Annual Convention of the Protestant Episcopal Church* (Savannah, GA: Power Press of John M. Cooper and Company, 1861), Papers of Stephen Elliott, 8.

89. McClain, *James Hervey Otey of Tennessee*, James Hervey Otey Papers.

90. James H. Otey, *Proceedings of a Convention of the Trustees of a Proposed University for the Southern States, under the Auspices of the Protestant Episcopal Church, together with a Narrative, and the Address of the Rt. Rev. James H. Otey, D.D., Prepared under the Order of the Convention, by the Secretary* (Atlanta: C.R. Hanleiter, 1857), Box 39:33, Folder Early Papers, File 38–39, James Hervey Otey Papers.

91. James H. Otey, *Trust in God the Only Safety of Nations* and *Constitutional Government Founded upon the Recognition of God's Sovereignty*, two discourses (New York: Daniel Dana Jr., 1860), James Hervey Otey Papers, 41.

92. James H. Otey, *A Pastoral Letter to the Clergy and Laity of the Protestant Episcopal Church in the Diocese of Tennessee* (Memphis, TN: Hutton & Freligh, PRS, Southern Publishing House, 1861), James Hervey Otey Papers, 3.

93. Ibid., 4.

94. Ibid.

95. Ibid., 5.

96. Gunter, "Bedford County During the Civil War," 86.

97. Elliott, *Address of the Rt. Rev. Stephen Elliott, D.D. to the 39th Annual Convention*, 3–4.

98. Ibid., 5.

99. Stephen Elliott, *New Wine Not to Be Put into Old Bottles*, A Sermon Preached in Christ Church, Savannah, Georgia, on Friday, February 28, 1862, Being the Day of Humiliation, Fasting, and Prayer, Appointed by the President of the Confederate States (Savannah, GA: Steam Power Press of John M. Cooper & Company, 1862), "The Southern Homefront, 1861–1865," *Documenting the American South* (Chapel Hill: University of North Carolina, n.d.), Call Number 4149 Conf., Rare Book Collection, Internet Electronic Edition.

100. Ibid., 9.

101. Ibid., 12.

102. Stephen Elliott, *How to Renew Our National Strength*, A Sermon Preached in Christ Church, Savannah, Georgia, Friday, November 15, 1861, Being the Day of Humiliation, Fasting, and Prayer, Appointed by the President of the Confederate States (Savannah, GA: Steam Power Press of John M. Cooper & Company, 1861). Papers of Stephen Elliott, 9–10.

103. Ibid., 11–12.

104. Stephen Elliott, *Funeral Services at the Burial of the Right Rev. Leonidas Polk, D.D.*, St. Paul's Church, Augusta, Georgia, on June 29, 1864. Papers of Stephen Elliott, 16.

105. Stephen Elliott, *Extract from a Sermon Preached on the 18th of September 1862, Containing a Tribute to the Privates of the Confederate Army*, "The Southern

Homefront, 1861–1865," *Documenting the American South* (Chapel Hill: University of North Carolina, n.d.), Call Number 4141 Conf. Rare Book Collection, Internet Electronic Edition.

106. Gilpin-Faust, *Creation of Confederate Nationalism*, 60.

107. Noll, "The Bible and Slavery," 49.

108. Elliott, *Address of the Rt. Rev. Stephen Elliott, D.D. to the 39th Annual Convention*, 10.

109. Noll, "The Bible and Slavery," 65.

110. Genovese, *A Consuming Fire*, 4. Genovese contends that Southern clergy masterfully concentrated on the numerous biblical references to portray slaveholding as a biblical way of life. They managed to separate slavery from race, not exploiting their view of the Noahic curse.

111. Ibid., 4.

112. Charles T. Quintard, *The Confederate Soldiers Manuel of Devotions*, Reel 1, RG 39:34, Box 90A, Quintard Papers.

113. Genovese, *A Consuming Fire*, 71.

114. Stephen Elliott, *Samson's Riddle*, A Sermon Preached in Christ Church, Savannah, Georgia, on Friday, March 27, 1863, Being the Day of Humiliation, Fasting and Prayer, Appointed by the President of the Confederate States (Macon, GA: Burke, Boykin & Company, Steam Book and Job Printers, 1863), "The Southern Homefront, 1861–1865," *Documenting the American South* (Chapel Hill: University of North Carolina, n.d.), Call Number 4151 Conf., Rare Book Collection, Internet Electronic Edition.

115. Ibid., 17.

116. Stephen Elliott, *Vain Is the Help of Man*, A Sermon Preached in Christ Church, Savannah, Georgia, on Thursday, September 15, 1864, Being the Day of Fasting, Humiliation, and Prayer, Appointed by the Governor of the State of Georgia (Macon, GA: Burke, Boykin, & Company, Steam Book and Job Printers, 1864), "The Southern Homefront, 1861–1865," *Documenting the American South* (Chapel Hill: University of North Carolina, n.d.), Call Number 4153 Conf. Rare Book Collection, Internet Electronic Edition.

117. Ibid., 7.

118. Stephen Elliott, *Ezra's Dilemma*, A Sermon Preached in Christ Church, Savannah, Georgia, on Friday August 21, 1863, Being the Day of Humiliation, Fasting, and Prayer, Appointed by the President of the Confederate States (Savannah, Georgia: Power Press of George N. Nichols, 1863). Papers of Stephen Elliott, 8.

119. Elliott, *Vain Is the Help of Man*, 8.
120. Burrows, *Shiloh: A Sermon*.
121. Ibid., 3.
122. Ibid., 3,4.
123. Ibid., 4.
124. Ibid.
125. Ibid., 7.
126. Pierce, *The Word of God a Nation's Life*.
127. Ibid., 8.
128. Chesebrough, *God Ordained This War*, 10.
129. Chesebrough, *Clergy Dissent in the Old South*, 26–27.

Chapter 4

130. Miller, Stout and Wilson, *Religion and the American Civil War*, 4.
131. Lincoln, Second Inaugural Address.
132. Romero, *Religion in the Rebel Ranks*, 128.
133. Norton, *Religion in Tennessee*, 70.
134. Norton, *Rebel Religion*, 52.
135. Fleming, *Civil War and Reconstruction in Alabama*, 224.
136. Charles Todd Quintard, Charles Todd Quintard: First Vice-Chancellor of the University, Box 39:34, Folder Biographical, Quintard Papers, 35.
137. Ibid., 36.
138. Charles Todd Quintard, Box 39:34, Folder 1863/1864/1865/1866, Quintard Papers.
139. Ibid.
140. Charles Todd Quintard, *Balm for the Weary: In Memory of Captain Thomas Edward King of Roswell Georgia who fell at the Battle of Chickamauga, Saturday September 19, 1863* (Columbia, SC: Evans & Cogswell Printers, 1864), Box 39:34, Folder 1863/1864/1865/1866, Quintard Papers, 7–8.
141. Charles Todd Quintard, *The Confederate Soldier's Pocket Manual of Devotions* (Charleston, SC: Evans & Cogswell, 1863), Tennessee State Library and Archives, *Civil War Collection (1861–1865)*, Mf. Ac. No. 824, Reel 3, Box 2, Folder 5.
142. Ibid., "The Litany," 29.
143. Ibid., "P.M. Our Rest," 81-82.
144. Hogan, Information Extracted from the Correspondence and Journal of Henry Hogan, 5.

145. Ibid., 6.
146. Ibid.
147. Ibid.
148. R.F. Bunting, Letter Written by the Chaplain of Terry's Regiment of the Texas Rangers on February 21, 1862, to E.H. Cushing and Distributed to the Army, Eighth Texas Cavalry, Stones River National Battlefield Regimental Files.
149. Ibid., Letter Written on January 4, 1862.
150. Ibid., Letter Written on January 10, 1862.
151. Ibid., Letter Written on June 3, 1863, 2.
152. Ibid., Letter Written on March 20, 1862.
153. Ibid.
154. Ibid., Letter Written on November 11, 1862.
155. Ibid., Letter Written on April 3, 1863, 6.
156. Ibid., Letter Written on November 11, 1862, 6.
157. Ibid., Letter Written on March 20, 1862, 3.
158. Ibid., 4.
159. Ibid., Letter Written on July 8, 1863, 6–7.
160. Ibid., Letter Written on June 3, 1863, 2.
161. Lizza Beall Deavenport, daughter of Reverend Thomas Hopkins Deavenport, Thomas Hopkins Deavenport Diary, Tennessee State Library and Archives, *Civil War Collection (1861–1865)*, Mf.Ac.No.824, Reel 2.
162. Larry Arnett, "Deavenport's Diary," *Tennessee Magazine*, Stones River National Battlefield Regimental Files. Folder Third Tennessee Infantry, folder contains article as well as the diary.
163. Thomas Hopkins Deavenport, Diary, Tennessee State Library and Archives, *Civil War Collection (1861–1865)*, Mf.Ac.No.824, Reel 2.
164. Ibid.
165. Ibid.
166. Arnett, "Deavenport's Diary."
167. Deavenport, Diary, Tennessee State Library and Archives.
168. John Johnston, Tennessee State Library and Archives, *Civil War Collection (1861–1865)*, Mf. Ac. No. 824, Reel Five, Memoirs, Box 13 Folder 9, 172.
169. Wyeth, *That Devil Forrest*, 558.
170. Ibid.
171. Ibid., 23.
172. Johnston, Tennessee State Library and Archives, 172.
173. Wyeth, *That Devil Forrest*, 558–59.

174. Ibid., 40.

175. Elliott, *Ezra's Dilemma*, 17.

176. Genovese, *A Consuming Fire*, 48.

CHAPTER 5

177. Whiteaker, "Civil War," *Tennessee Encyclopedia of History and Culture.*

178. Stephen Elliott, *Extract from a Sermon Preached on the 18th of September 1862, Containing a Tribute to the Privates of the Confederate Army,* "The Southern Homefront, 1861–1865," *Documenting the American South* (Chapel Hill: University of North Carolina, n.d.), Call Number 4141 Conf. Rare Book Collection, Internet Electronic Edition.

179. Shelby Foote in Ken Burns, *The Civil War*, Episode II, "A Very Bloody Affair: 1862."

180. Romero, *Religion in the Rebel Ranks*, 40.

181. Silver, *Confederate Morale*, 129.

182. James Caswell Edenton, Tennessee State Library and Archives, *Civil War Collection (1861–1865)*, Mf.Ac.No.824, Reel 2, Box 6, Folder 9, August 27, 1861.

183. Stones River National Battlefield Regimental Files, Terry's Texas Rangers, Eighth Texas Cavalry Folder.

184. E.H. Ross, Letter Written on June 28, 1862 to Ross's Family, Stones River National Battlefield Regimental Files. Folder, Terry's Texas Rangers, Eighth Texas Cavalry, Company A.

185. Ibid., Letter Written on October 22, 1861.

186. Johnston, Tennessee State Library and Archives, 2.

187. Ibid., 13.

188. Ibid., 31.

189. Ibid., 162.

190. Ibid., 180.

191. Ibid.

192. Ibid., 1., Psalm. 37:25 KJV.

193. James L. Cooper, Diary, April 13, 1862, Tennessee State Library and Archives, *Civil War Collection (1861–1865)*, Mf.Ac.No.824, Reel 5, Box 12, Folder 11.

194. Ibid., August 5, 1866.

195. Ibid., December 31, 1862.

196. Ibid., March 1864.

197. Craddock, "Sam Davis," *Tennessee Encyclopedia of History and Culture*.

198. Sam Davis, Tennessee State Library and Archives, *Civil War Collection (1861–1865)*, Mf.Ac.No.824, Military Personnel, Reel 6, Box 15, Folder 8.

199. Ibid.

200. Carrol H. Clark, Stones River National Battlefield Regimental Files. Folder Sixteenth Tennessee Infantry, CSA. The original diary was lost. This is a photocopy of a reprint of articles written for the *Spencer Times* in 1911, which were based on the diaries.

201. Ibid., 19.

202. James J. Womack, Diary, May 14, 1862, Stones River National Battlefield Regimental Files. Sixteenth Tennessee Infantry, CSA, photocopy of entire diary.

203. Ibid., June 9, 1861.

204. Ibid., May 21, 1862.

205. William A. Brown, Stones River National Battlefield Regimental Files. Mississippi, Stanford's Battery, CSA. Entries from Brown's notebook for the period of November 1861 to December 1864, 18–19.

206. Ibid., 141.

207. Ibid., 156.

208. J.W. Harmon, Memoirs, Tennessee State Library and Archives, *Civil War Collection (1861–1865)*, Mf.Ac.No.824, Reel 5, Box 13, Folder 6, 3.

209. Ibid., 25.

210. Ibid.

211. Ibid.

212. Ibid.

213. Watkins, *Company Aytch*, ix.

214. Ibid., 81.

215. Ibid., 84.

216. Ibid., 107.

217. Ibid., 108.

218. Ibid., 127.

219. Ibid., ix.

220. Stephen A. Jordan, Tennessee State Library and Archives, *Civil War Collection (1861–1865)*, Mf.Ac.No.824, Diaries, Box 6, Folder 14, December 24, 1863 and December 29, 1864.

221. Joseph R. Mothershead, Tennessee State Library and Archives, *Civil War Collection (1861–1865)*, Mf.Ac.No.824, Diaries, Box 7, Folder 5, June 10, 1862.

222. William Mebane Pollard, Tennessee State Library and Archives, *Civil War Collection (1861-1865)*, Mf.Ac.No.824, Diaries, Box 7, Folder 6, March 16, 1862.

223. Chas R. Donoho, Letter to James Brickell Murfree, Tennessee State Library and Archives, *Civil War Collection (1861–1865)*, Mf.Ac.No.824, Reel 4, Box 10, Folder 32.

224. Henry Melville Doak, Tennessee State Library and Archives, *Civil War Collection (1861–1865)*, Mf.Ac.No.824, Reel 5, Box 12, Folder 13.

225. F.J. Paine, Tennessee State Library and Archives, *Civil War Collection (1861–1865)*, Mf.Ac.No.824, Reel 4, Box 11, Folder 2.

226. Andrew Rice, Tennessee State Library and Archives, *Civil War Collection (1861–1865)*, Mf.Ac.No.824, Reel 4, Box 11, Folder 11.

227. William J. Rogers, Stones River National Battlefield Regimental Files. Thirteenth Tennessee Infantry, CSA, From the West Tennessee Historical Society Papers, Diary Covers June 1862–May 1863, May 10, 1863.

228. Ibid., March 16, 1863, 83.

229. Joseph Anderson Rogers, Tennessee State Library and Archives, *Civil War Collection (1861–1865)*, Mf.Ac.No.824, Reel 4, Box 11, Folder 14.

230. William Harbot Sugg, Tennessee State Library and Archives, *Civil War Collection (1861–1865)*, Mf.Ac.No.824, Reel 4, Box 11, Folder 25.

231. Thomas R. Hooper, Stones River National Battlefield Regimental Files. Sixteenth Tennessee Infantry, CSA. Photocopy of Diary, December 28, 1862.

232. W.H. Williams, Tennessee State Library and Archives, *Civil War Collection (1861–1865)*, Mf.Ac.No824, Reel 4, Box 11, Folder 42.

233. Joseph E. Johnston, contained in the memoirs of R.W. Banks, Tennessee State Library and Archives, *Civil War Collection (1861–1865)*, Mf.Ac. No.824, Reel 4, Box 12, Folder 2.

234. R.W. Banks, Tennessee State Library and Archives, *Civil War Collection (1861–1865)*, Mf.Ac.No.824, Reel 4, Box 12, Folder 2.

235. Rennolds, *History of the Henry County Commands*, 75.

236. Chesebrough, *God Ordained This War*, 3.

237. George Thompson Blakemore, Tennessee State Library and Archives, *Civil War Collection (1861–1865)*, Mf.Ac.No.824, Reel 2, 2.

238. Genovese, *A Consuming Fire*, 45.

Chapter 6

239. James M. McPherson, "Afterword" in Miller, Stout and Wilson, *Religion and the American Civil War*, 409.

240. Romero, *Religion in the Rebel Ranks*, 131.

241. Paludan, "Religion and the American Civil War," in *Religion and the American Civil War*, ed. Miller, Stout and Wilson, 36.

242. Miller, Stout and Wilson, *Religion and the American Civil War*, 18.

243. Psalm 46:1, KJV (King James Version).

Selected Bibliography

Primary Sources

Burrows, John Lansing. *Shiloh: A Sermon*. Chapel Hill: University of North Carolina. Call number 4849 Conf. Rare Book Collection. Internet Electronic Edition.

Davis, Jefferson. "Farewell to the United States Senate." January 21, 1861. *The Rise and Fall of the Confederate Government*, Vol. 1, 221–25, 1958 reprint edition.

———. "Inaugural Address as Provisional President of the Confederacy." Montgomery, Alabama, February 18, 1861. CSA Congressional Journal, 1:64–66, as reprinted in Lynda L. Crist and Mary S. Dix, eds. *The Papers of Jefferson Davis*. Baton Rouge: Louisiana State University Press, 1992. 7:46-50.

———. "Speech at Richmond." June 1, 1861. Spotswood Hotel, Richmond, Virginia. Houston, TX: Rice University. Internet Electronic Edition.

Elliott, Stephen (1806–1866). Papers of Stephen Elliott. University Archives and Special Collections, The University of the South, Sewanee, Tennessee.

———. "The Southern Homefront, 1861–1865." In *Documenting the American South*. Chapel Hill: University of North Carolina. Internet Electronic Edition.

Ewell, Richard S. *The Making of a Soldier: Letters of General R.S. Ewell*. Ed. by Percy Gatling Hamlin. Whittet & Shepperson, 1935. As reprinted in Time-Life, ed. *Decoying the Yanks: Jackson's Valley Campaign*. *The Civil War*. Alexandria, VA: Time-Life Books, 1984.

Fulkerson, Abram. Letter to Wife, Selina, Regarding the Death of Stonewall Jackson. May 18, 1863. Virginia Military Institute Archives. Fulkerson Family Papers. Manuscript #0363. Internet Electronic Edition.

Hogan, Henry Daniel Polk. Information Extracted from the Correspondence and Journal of Henry Hogan by Gerald A. Miller and Helen Williams Miller (granddaughter of Henry Daniel Polk Hogan), and Compiled in "Reverend Henry Daniel Polk Hogan (1840–1930) and Clara Dill Hogan (1853–1906)." National Park Service. Stones River National Battlefield. Also Confederate Civil War Military Records, Roll 217 microfilm, Record Group M268, National Archives, Washington, D.C.

Jackson, Thomas Jonathan (1824–1863). Stonewall Jackson Papers (1844–1863). Virginia Military Institute Archives. Internet Electronic Edition.

Lincoln, Abraham. Second Inaugural Address. March 4, 1865. OurDocuments.gov. Internet Electronic Edition.

Otey, James H (1800–1863). *James Hervey Otey Papers*. University Archives and Special Collections, The University of the South, Sewanee, Tennessee.

Pierce, George Foster. *The Word of God a Nation's Life*. A Sermon Preached Before the Bible Convention of the Confederate States. Augusta, Georgia, March 19, 1862. Chapel Hill: University of North Carolina Press. Call Number 4179. Conf. Rare Book Collection. Internet Electronic Edition.

Polk, Leonidas (1806–1864). Polk Papers. University Archives and Special Collections, The University of the South, Sewanee, Tennessee.

Quintard, Charles Todd (1824–1898). Quintard Papers. University Archives and Special Collections, The University of the South, Sewanee, Tennessee.

Rennolds, Lieutenant Edwin H. *A History of the Henry County Commands*. Jacksonville, FL: Sun Publishing Company, 1904. Reprint, Kennesaw, GA: Continental Book Company, 1961.

Smith, Major General F.H. Letter on the Death of Stonewall Jackson. General Order No. 30, and General Order No. 31. Virginia Military Institute. May 11, 13, 14, 1863. Virginia Military Institute Archives. Internet Electronic Edition.

Stones River National Battlefield Regimental Files. National Park Service. Murfreesboro, Tennessee.

Taylor, General Richard. *Destruction and Reconstruction: Personal Experiences of the Late War*. New York: D. Appleton and Company, 1879. As reprinted in Time-Life, ed. *Decoying the Yanks: Jackson's Valley Campaign. The Civil War*. Alexandria, VA: Time-Life Books, 1984.

Tennessee State Library and Archives. *Civil War Collection (1861–1865)*. Mf.Ac.No.824.

Watkins, Sam. *Company Aytch: Or a Side Show of the Big Show*. Edited by M. Thomas Inge. New York: A Plume Book, 1999.

Wyeth, John Allan. Foreword by Albert Castel, ed. *That Devil Forrest: Life of General Nathan Bedford Forrest*. Baton Rouge: Louisiana State University Press, 1959, 1987, 1989.

Secondary Sources

Ayers, Edward L. "A Review of Randall M. Miller, Harry S. Stout, and Charles Reagan Wilson, eds., *Religion and the American Civil War*." *Journal of Southern Religion*. Internet Electronic Edition.

Boles, John B. *The Irony of Southern Religion*. New York: Peter Lang, 1994.

Burns, Ken. *The Civil War*. Produced by Ken Burns and Ric Burns. Public Broadcasting Station Production Company. Release Fall 1990. Episode II, "A Very Bloody Affair: 1862."

Chesebrough, David B. *Clergy Dissent in the Old South, 1830–1865*. Carbondale: Southern Illinois University Press, 1996.

———. *God Ordained This War: Sermons on the Sectional Crisis, 1830–1865*. Columbia: University of South Carolina Press, 1991.

Craddock, Patrick. "Sam Davis." In *The Tennessee Encyclopedia of History and Culture*. Internet Electronic Edition.

Davis, William C., Brian C. Pohanka and Don Troiani eds. *Civil War Journal: The Leaders*. Nashville, TN: Rutledge Hill Press, 1997.

Fellman, Michael. *The Making of Robert E. Lee*. New York: Random House, 2000.

Fleming, Walter L. *Civil War and Reconstruction in Alabama*. New York: Peter Smith, 1949.

Genovese, Eugene D. *A Consuming Fire: The Fall of the Confederacy in the Mind of the White Christian South*. Athens: University of Georgia Press, 1998.

Gilpin-Faust, Drew. *The Creation of Confederate Nationalism: Ideology and Identity in the Civil War South*. Baton Rouge: Louisiana State University Press, 1988.

Gunter, Charles Raymond, Jr. "Bedford County During the Civil War." Master's thesis, University of Tennessee, 1963.

Heyrman, Christine Leigh. *Southern Cross: The Beginnings of the Bible Belt*. Chapel Hill: University of North Carolina Press, 1997.

McClain, Frank M. *James Hervey Otey of Tennessee*. Series *Builders for Christ*. The National Council. New York, 1956. Box 39:33, Folder Correspondence 1860–1863. RG 39:33-17. University Archives and Special Collections, University of the South, Sewanee, Tennessee.

McMillan, Malcolm C. *The Alabama Confederate Reader*. Tuscaloosa: University of Alabama Press, 1963.

Miller, Randall M., Harry S. Stout and Charles Reagan Wilson, eds. *Religion and the American Civil War*. New York: Oxford University Press, 1998.

Norton, Herman. *Rebel Religion*. St. Louis, MO: Bethany Press, 1961.

———. *Religion in Tennessee: 1777–1945*. Knoxville: University of Tennessee Press, 1981.

Rable, George C. *God's Almost Chosen Peoples: A Religious History of the American Civil War*. Chapel Hill: University of North Carolina Press, 2010.

Robertson, James I., Jr. *Stonewall Jackson: The Man, the Soldier, the Legend*. New York: MacMillan Publishing, 1997.

Romero, Sidney J. *Religion in the Rebel Ranks*. New York: University Press of America, 1983.

Silver, James W. *Confederate Morale and Church Propaganda*. Gloucester, MA: Peter Smith, 1957.

Whiteaker, Larry H. "Civil War." In *The Tennessee Encyclopedia of History and Culture*. Internet Electronic Edition.

Index

About the Authors

Traci Nichols-Belt is an ordained and licensed minister and holds a master's degree in history from Middle Tennessee State University and a bachelor's degree in political science from Anderson University. During her academic career at MTSU, Traci worked for the Tennessee State Museum and wrote two National Register nominations for the Johnsonville Historic District in New Johnsonville, Tennessee, and the Historical AME Church and Cemeteries in Alexandria, Tennessee. Traci has also worked as a historical consultant and grant writer for the Clement Railroad Hotel and Museum in Dickson, Tennessee. Traci's article "Chaplains in the Army of Tennessee, CSA: Warring Disciples Carrying the Gospel" was published in the Winter 2004 issue of the *Tennessee Historical Quarterly*. Additionally, she wrote a review of Sam Davis Elliot's book, *Doctor Quintard Chaplain CSA and Second Bishop of Tennessee*, for the Spring 2004 issue of the *Tennessee Historical Quarterly*.

Gordon T. Belt is an information professional specializing in local archives, historical research and government and public policy. He currently works as the library manager for the First Amendment Center at Vanderbilt University in Nashville, Tennessee, and has written several articles for the First Amendment Center website on legislative issues and history. Gordon holds a master's degree in history from Middle Tennessee State University and a bachelor's degree in political science from the University of Tennessee at Chattanooga. He is an active member in the Society of Tennessee Archivists and holds memberships in the Society of American Archivists, Special Libraries Association, National Council on Public History and the Tennessee Historical Society. Gordon is also the founding editor and publisher of *The Posterity Project*, an award-winning blog devoted to issues related to archives, history, civic responsibility and open access to public records in his home state of Tennessee.